Contents

Introduction

The contents of this book are based upon the National Science Education Standards for Grade 8. These standards include (A) Science as Inquiry, (B) Physical Science, (C) Life Science, (D) Earth and Space Science, (E) Science and Technology, (F) Science in Personal and Social Perspectives, and (G) History and Nature of Science.

This book will help teachers, students, parents, and tutors. Teachers can use this book either to introduce or review a topic in their science classroom. Students will find the book useful in reviewing the major concepts in science. Parents can use this book to help their children with topics that may be posing a problem in the classroom. Tutors can use this book as a basis for their lessons and for assigning questions and activities.

This book includes ten lessons that focus on the ten major concepts presented in the content standards: Physical Science, Life Science, and Earth and Space Science. The lessons also cover the twelve major concepts presented in the other standards. A table on page 4 provides a correlation between the contents of each lesson and the National Science Education Standards.

Before beginning the book, the reader can check his or her knowledge of the content by completing the *Assessment*. The *Assessment* consists of questions that deal with the content standards. This will allow the reader to determine how much he or she knows about a particular concept before beginning to read about it. The *Assessment* may also serve as a way of leading the reader to a specific lesson that may be of special interest.

Each lesson follows the same sequence in presenting the material. A list of *Key Terms* is always provided at the beginning of each lesson. This list includes all the boldfaced terms and their definitions presented in the same order that they are introduced in the lesson. The reader can develop a sense of the lesson content by glancing through the *Key Terms*. Each lesson then provides background information about the concept. This information is divided into several sections. Each section is written so that the reader is not overwhelmed with details. Rather, the reader is guided through the concept in a logical sequence. Each lesson then moves on to a *Review*. This section consists of several multiple-choice and short-answer questions. The multiple-choice questions check if the reader has retained information that was covered in the lesson. The short-answer questions check if the reader can use information from the lesson to provide the answers.

Each lesson then moves on to a series of activities. These activities are designed to check the reader's understanding of the information. Some activities extend the lesson by presenting additional information. The activities are varied so as not to be boring. For example, reading passages about interesting and unusual findings are included. Questions to check reading comprehension are then asked. As a change of pace, some activities are meant to engage the reader in a "fun-type" exercise. These activities include crosswords, word searches, jumbled letters, and cryptograms.

The last activity in each lesson is an experiment. Each experiment has been designed so that the required items are easy to locate and can usually be found in most households. Care has been taken to avoid the use of any dangerous materials or chemicals. However, an adult should always be present when a student is conducting an experiment. In some cases, the experimental procedure reminds students that adult supervision is required. Before beginning any experiment, an adult should review the list of materials and the procedure. In this way, the adult will be aware of any situations that may need special attention. The adult should review the safety issues before the experiment is begun. The adult may want to check a laboratory manual for specific safety precautions that should be followed when doing an experiment, such as wearing safety goggles and never touching or tasting chemicals.

The book then follows with a *Science Fair* section. Information is presented on how to conduct and present a science fair project. In some cases, the experiment at the end of a lesson can serve as the basis for a science fair project. Additional suggestions are also provided with advice on how to choose an award-winning science fair project.

A *Glossary* is next. This section lists all the boldfaced terms in alphabetical order and indicates the page on which the term is used. The book concludes with an *Answer Key*, which gives the answers to all the activity questions, including the experiment.

This book has been designed and written so that teachers, students, parents, and tutors will find it easy to use and follow. Most importantly, students will benefit from this book by achieving at a higher level in class and on standardized tests.

National Science Education Standards

Standard A: SCIENCE AS INQUIRY

A1 Abilities necessary to do scientific inquiry
A2 Understandings about scientific inquiry

Standard B: PHYSICAL SCIENCE

B1 Properties and changes of properties in matter
B2 Motions and forces
B3 Transfer of energy

Standard C: LIFE SCIENCE

C1 Structure and function in living systems
C2 Reproduction and heredity
C3 Regulation and behavior
C4 Populations and ecosystems
C5 Diversity and adaptations of organisms

Standard D: EARTH AND SPACE SCIENCE

D1 Earth's history and structure
D2 Earth in the solar system

Standard E: SCIENCE AND TECHNOLOGY

E1 Abilities of technological design
E2 Understandings about science and technology

Standard F: SCIENCE IN PERSONAL AND SOCIAL PERSPECTIVES

F1 Personal health
F2 Populations, resources, and environments
F3 Natural hazards
F4 Risks and benefits
F5 Science and technology in society

Standard G: HISTORY AND NATURE OF SCIENCE

G1 Science as a human endeavor
G2 Nature of science
G3 History of science

National Science Education Standards
Science 8, SV 9781419034367

Correlation to National Science Education Standards

Unit 1: Physical Science
Lesson 1: Properties and Changes of Properties in Matter
Background
  Information B1, E1, E2, F5, G1, G2, G3
Review. B1
Solubility. B1
Density B1
Chemical Reactions B1
Experiment: Conservation of Mass A1, A2, B1, G2

Lesson 2: Motions and Forces
Background Information B2, E2, G3
Review B2, E2, G3
Motion B2
A Roller-Coaster Ride B2, E1, E2, F4, F5, G1, G2
A Newtonian Crossword Puzzle. B2, G3
Experiment: Acceleration Due to Gravity A1, A2, B2, G3

Lesson 3: Transfer of Energy
Background
  Information B3, E1, E2, F2, F3, F4, F5, G3
Review. B3
Chemical Reactions and Energy I. B3
Chemical Reactions and Energy II B3
A Long Voyage B3, E1, E2, F3, F4, F5, G1, G3
Experiment: A Model of Nuclear Fission A1, A2, B3, G2

Unit 2: Life Science
Lesson 4: Structure and Function in Living Systems
Background Information C1
Review. C1
When the Kidneys
  Don't Work C1, E1, E2, F1, F4, F5, G1, G2, G3
Hormones and Reproduction C1, F1
The Endocrine System C1, F1
Experiment: The Nervous System. A1, A2, C1

Lesson 5: Reproduction and Heredity
Background
  Information. C2, E1, E2, F1, F4, F5, G1, G2, G3
Review C2, F5
DNA Replication. C2
RNA Transcription. C2
Protein Synthesis C2
Mutations. C2
Experiment: Extracting DNA. A1, A2, C2

Lesson 6: Regulation and Behavior
Background Information C3
Review. C3
Focusing the Light C3, F1
Mathematics and the Senses. C3
It Doesn't Smell Anymore!. C3, F1
Experiment: What Do You Taste?. A1, A2, C3

Lesson 7: Populations and Ecosystems
Background Information C4, F2
Review C4, F2
A Population and Ecosystem
  Crossword Puzzle C4, F2
Population Growth. C4, F2
The Carbon Cycle C4, F2, G3
Experiment: Estimating the Size of
  a Population A1, A2. C4. F2, G2

Lesson 8: Diversity and Adaptations of Organisms
Background Information C5, F2, G1, G2, G3
Review C5, G3
The Galápagos Finches C5, F2, G3
Weight as an Adaptation C5, F1, F4
Another Theory of Evolution C5, G3
Experiment: Natural Selection A1, A2, C5, F2, F4

Unit 3: Earth and Space Science
Lesson 9: Earth's History and Structure
Background Information D1, E1, E2, F3, G3
Review. D1
Tectonic Plates. D1, F3
Complete the Sentences D1
Seismic Waves. D1, E2, F3
The Richter Scale D1, E1, E2, F3, F5, G3
Experiment: Convection Currents A1, A2, D1, F3

Lesson 10: Earth in the Solar System
Background Information D2, G1, G3
Review. D2, G3
The Moon's Orbit B2, D2
Kepler's Laws. D2, G3
Squeeze Gently D2, E1, E2, F5, G3
The Sun D2
Experiment: Calculating the Distance
  to the Sun A1, A2, D2, G1, G3

Assessment

Darken the circle by the best answer.

1. A sample of silver has a mass of 21 grams and a volume of 2 cm³. What is the density of silver?

   Ⓐ 21 g/cm³

   Ⓑ 10.5 g/cm³

   Ⓒ 2 g/cm3

   Ⓓ 1.05 g/cm³

2. Examine the following chemical equation, which shows only the reactants.

   $Na_2O + H_2O \rightarrow$

   How many Na atoms must be present in the product that is formed?

   Ⓐ 1

   Ⓑ 2

   Ⓒ 3

   Ⓓ 4

3. What two factors affect the force of a moving object?

   Ⓐ mass and acceleration

   Ⓑ speed and distance traveled

   Ⓒ velocity and speed

   Ⓓ mass and weight

4. Which of the following is associated with action-reaction pairs?

   Ⓐ Newton's first law of motion

   Ⓑ Newton's second law of motion

   Ⓒ Newton's third law of motion

   Ⓓ Newton's law of universal gravitation

5. Which of the following statements is true regarding an exothermic reaction?

   Ⓐ No energy is required to start the reaction.

   Ⓑ The products contain less energy than the reactants.

   Ⓒ The products contain more energy than the reactants.

   Ⓓ Energy is absorbed.

6. In the equation $E = mc^2$, c represents

   Ⓐ mass.

   Ⓑ the speed of light.

   Ⓒ motion.

   Ⓓ energy.

7. Which structure carries urine from the urinary bladder out the body?

   Ⓐ urethra

   Ⓑ ureter

   Ⓒ nephron

   Ⓓ fallopian tube

8. Which of the following terms is correctly paired?

   Ⓐ cerebrum—involuntary responses

   Ⓑ cerebellum—muscle coordination

   Ⓒ medulla—thinking

   Ⓓ peripheral nervous system—brain and spinal cord

Assessment page 2

9. Any change in DNA is called a

   Ⓐ disease.

   Ⓑ recombinant DNA.

   Ⓒ mutation.

   Ⓓ double helix.

10. Identify the structure that contains cones and rods.

   Ⓐ retina

   Ⓑ lens

   Ⓒ optic nerve

   Ⓓ skin

11. Which is an example of how homeostasis operates?

   Ⓐ A furnace turns on during a summer day.

   Ⓑ A car's engine shuts off after it is parked.

   Ⓒ A sprinkler system turns on when it is raining.

   Ⓓ An air conditioner turns on during a hot day in August.

12. Which process adds carbon dioxide to the atmosphere?

   Ⓐ respiration

   Ⓑ evaporation

   Ⓒ transpiration

   Ⓓ photosynthesis

13. A feature that increases an organism's chance of survival is known as a(n)

   Ⓐ vestigial structure.

   Ⓑ reproductive structure.

   Ⓒ adaptation.

   Ⓓ inherited trait.

14. What type of boundary forms when two continental plates move apart from one another?

   Ⓐ convergent boundary

   Ⓑ divergent boundary

   Ⓒ transform boundary

   Ⓓ oceanic-oceanic crust boundary

15. Earth's crust and the upper part of the mantle make up the

   Ⓐ asthenosphere.

   Ⓑ core.

   Ⓒ atmosphere.

   Ⓓ lithosphere.

16. During a lunar eclipse,

   Ⓐ the sun's shadow falls on Earth.

   Ⓑ Earth's shadow falls on the sun.

   Ⓒ Earth's shadow falls on the moon.

   Ⓓ the moon's shadow falls on Earth.

Lesson 1 Properties and Changes of Properties in Matter

If you look closely, you will see changes taking place all around you. Some of these changes happen quickly. Perhaps the wind suddenly picks up and blows the leaves across the lawn. Other changes happen slowly. Perhaps the leaves on the trees are gradually turning color as the weather gets colder. In this lesson, you will learn that scientists recognize two types of changes. However, these two types do not depend on how quickly

Key Terms

matter—anything that has both volume and mass

volume—the amount of space taken up, or occupied, by an object

mass—the amount of matter in an object

physical property—property of matter that can be observed or measured without changing the matter's identity

density—the ratio of the mass of a substance to the volume of the substance

melting point—the temperature at which a solid melts to form a liquid

boiling point—the temperature at which a liquid boils to form a gas

solubility—the ability of one substance to dissolve in another substance

solution—a mixture made by dissolving one substance in another substance

chemical property—property that describes matter based on its ability to change into new matter that has different properties

reactivity—the ability of one substance to interact chemically with another substance

physical change—a change that does not change the identity of a substance

chemical change—a change that results in the change of the identity of a substance

chemical reaction—a process in which one or more substances change to make one or more new substances

exothermic reaction—a chemical reaction that releases energy

chemical equation—a shorthand method to show what happens during a chemical reaction

reactant—a substance that reacts with another substance in a chemical reaction

product—the substance that is made during a chemical reaction

endothermic reaction—a chemical reaction that absorbs energy

chemical formula—a shorthand way to use chemical symbols and numbers to represent a substance

atom—the basic building block of matter

law of conservation of mass—the law that states that mass cannot be created or destroyed during ordinary physical and chemical changes

or slowly they take place. Rather, they depend on what happens to the substance that changes.

Matter

The leaves that blow across a lawn or change color in the fall are an example of matter. In fact, everything that you can see is an example of matter. This includes a star you see in the night sky, this book you are reading, and you whose reflection you can see in a mirror. Scientists define **matter** as anything that has both volume and mass. **Volume** is the amount of space that is taken up, or occupied, by an object. For example, the volume of this book is the amount of space it takes up on a book shelf or in your backpack. **Mass** is the amount of matter in an object. Because it has many more pages, a dictionary has more mass than this book.

Physical Properties

Both volume and mass are examples of physical properties of matter. A **physical property** of matter can be observed or measured without changing the matter's identity. You can determine the volume of this book by measuring its length, width, and height. If you multiply these three values, you will get the volume of this book. You can determine the mass of this book by using a balance.

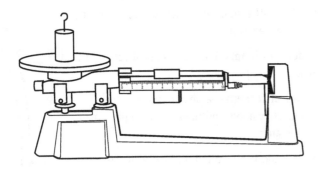

Density

Another physical property is density. **Density** is the ratio of mass to volume. The equation for density is written as follows.

$$\text{density} = \frac{\text{mass}}{\text{volume}} \text{ or } D = \frac{m}{V}$$

Units for density consist of a mass unit divided by a volume unit. Some units for density are g/cm^3, g/mL, and kg/m^3.

The density of pure gold is 19.3 g/cm^3. However, if you were to calculate the density of a piece of 18 carat gold jewelry, you would find that its density is not 19.3 g/cm^3. The density of 18 carat gold jewelry is not the same as pure gold because 18 carat gold is not pure. Other metals are added to make 18 carat gold jewelry. The density of 18 carat gold depends on the materials that have been added.

Density is a useful physical property for identifying substances. Each substance has a density that differs from the densities of other substances. Moreover, the density of a substance is always the same if the temperature and pressure do not change.

Boiling Point and Melting Point

Melting point and boiling point are also physical properties of a substance. A substance's **melting point** is the temperature at which the solid substance melts to form a liquid. The melting point of water is 0°C (32°F). A substance's **boiling point** is the temperature at which a liquid substance boils to form a gas. The boiling point of water is 100°C (212°F).

Like density, melting and boiling points can be used to identify a substance. For example, if a colorless liquid boils at 78.4°C, you know that it is not water. If you refer to a table that lists the boiling points of different substances, you would find that ethanol boils at 78.4°C. Therefore, the colorless liquid might be ethanol. However, to be sure, you must test other properties of the colorless liquid before you can conclude that it is ethanol.

Solubility

Solubility is the ability of one substance to dissolve in another substance. Solubility is another physical property that can be used to identify a substance.

Sugar dissolves in water. Therefore sugar is said to be soluble in water. When sugar is dissolved in water, it forms a solution. A **solution** is usually made by dissolving a solid in a liquid so that the two substances are evenly mixed.

Potassium carbonate and potassium sulfate are white, powdery substances that are used in fertilizers. Because both compounds are white powders, you cannot distinguish between the two compounds by looking at them. However, potassium carbonate is ten times more soluble in water than potassium sulfate. Therefore, you can identify them by measuring how much of each substance dissolves in a given volume of water. The one that dissolves more in a given volume is potassium carbonate.

Chemical Properties

Physical properties are not the only properties that describe matter. **Chemical properties** describe matter based on its ability to change into new matter that has different properties. A chemical property of wood is its flammability. When wood burns, new substances are produced. These include ashes and gases. These new substances have very different properties than the wood.

Another chemical property is reactivity. **Reactivity** is the ability of one substance to interact chemically with another substance. Reactivity is usually described in terms of chemical reactions, which you will study later in this lesson.

Unlike physical properties, chemical properties are not as easy to observe. For example, you know that wood is flammable. However, you cannot observe this chemical property until the wood is burning.

Physical and Chemical Changes

A **physical change** is a change that does not change the identity of a substance. Examples of physical changes include melting ice, tearing a piece of paper, and breaking a pencil. Physical changes cause a change in the physical characteristics of a substance, such as its volume, mass, or temperature.

A **chemical change** results in a change in the identity of a substance. If you mix a colorless liquid with another colorless liquid and the two liquids produce a yellow solid, you know that a chemical change has occurred. The identities of the original substances have been changed. When a chemical change occurs, the process by which new substances are formed is called a **chemical reaction**.

Changes in Energy

A chemical reaction is always accompanied by a change in energy. Some chemical reactions release energy. These reactions are known as **exothermic reactions**. Exothermic reactions usually release energy as heat. The heat that is released by a chemical reaction can be measured as an increase in temperature. An example of an exothermic reaction occurs when you light a gas barbecue grill.

Propane is used in barbecue grills because propane burns in the presence of oxygen. When propane gas burns, carbon dioxide and water are formed. This reaction can be written as a chemical equation. A **chemical equation** is a shorthand method to show what happens during a chemical reaction. The following is the chemical equation that shows what happens when propane burns in oxygen.

$$C_3H_8 \ + \ O_2 \ \rightarrow \ H_2O \ + \ CO_2 \ + \ energy$$
propane   oxygen   water   carbon
                                dioxide

In this equation, propane and oxygen are reactants. A **reactant** is a substance that reacts with another substance in a chemical reaction. In this equation, water and carbon dioxide are the products. A **product** is the substance that is made during a chemical reaction.

www.harcourtschoolsupply.com
9
Lesson 1, Properties and Changes of Properties in Matter
Science 8, SV 9781419034367

Some reactions absorb energy. These reactions are known as **endothermic reactions**. For example, water can be split to form oxygen and hydrogen if electrical energy is added. The following chemical equation shows what happens in this reaction.

$$H_2O + energy \rightarrow H_2 + O_2$$
$$\text{water} \qquad\qquad \text{hydrogen} \quad \text{oxygen}$$

Conservation of Mass

Notice in the above equation that water is written as H_2O. This is the chemical formula for water. A **chemical formula** is a shorthand way to use chemical symbols and numbers to represent a substance. The chemical symbol for hydrogen is H. The chemical symbol for oxygen is O. The 2 in the formula indicates that water consists of 2 H atoms and 1 O atom. Notice that the number 1 is never written in a formula. An **atom** is the building block of matter.

Take another look at the above equation. Notice that there are 2 H atoms on the left side of the arrow. There are also 2 H atoms on the right side of the arrow. However, there is only 1 O atom on the left side of the arrow, while there are 2 O atoms on the right side of the arrow. This indicates that an oxygen

atom was created during this chemical reaction. However, mass cannot be created or destroyed during ordinary physical and chemical changes. This is known as the **law of conservation of mass**.

During a chemical reaction, atoms are just rearranged. Every atom in the reactants becomes part of the products. Therefore, the number of atoms in each element in the reactants must equal the number of atoms of those elements in the products. To do this, an equation must be balanced so that the law of conservation of mass is obeyed.

Balancing a chemical equation involves placing a number in front of a formula. You cannot balance an equation by changing any of the formulas. To balance the O atoms in the above equation, a 2 must be placed in front of H_2O.

$$2H_2O + energy \rightarrow H_2 + O_2$$

There are now 2 O atoms on each side. However, notice that there are now 4 H atoms on the left side ($2H_2O$) and only 2 H atoms on the right side (H_2). Therefore, a 2 must be placed in front of H_2.

$$2H_2O + energy \rightarrow 2H_2 + O_2$$

There are now 4 H atoms and 2 O atoms on each side. The law of conservation of mass is obeyed.

Lesson 1

Darken the circle by the best answer.

1. What two quantities must be known to calculate the density of a sample of matter?

   Ⓐ color and mass

   Ⓑ mass and volume

   Ⓒ length and mass

   Ⓓ solubility and mass

2. All chemical reactions involve a(n)

   Ⓐ release of energy.

   Ⓑ input of energy.

   Ⓒ creation of atoms.

   Ⓓ rearrangement of atoms.

3. A sample of lead has a mass of 33 grams and a volume of 3 cm^3. What is the density of lead?

   Ⓐ 99 g/cm^3

   Ⓑ 33 g/cm^3

   Ⓒ 11 g/cm^3

   Ⓓ 3 g/cm^3

4. Which of the following is an example of a chemical change?

   Ⓐ water evaporating

   Ⓑ ice cream melting

   Ⓒ wood burning

   Ⓓ face blushing

5. Examine the following chemical equation, which shows only the reactants.

$$Na_2O + H_2O \rightarrow$$

   How many O atoms must be present in the product that is formed?

   Ⓐ 1

   Ⓑ 2

   Ⓒ 3

   Ⓓ 4

6. Which of the following statements refers to a physical property of a substance?

   Ⓐ Carbon combines with oxygen to form carbon dioxide.

   Ⓑ Zinc metal reacts with an acid to produce hydrogen gas.

   Ⓒ The atoms in a substance can be rearranged to form a new substance.

   Ⓓ The density of copper is 8.93 g/cm^3.

7. Examine the following reaction.

$$2Na + Cl_2 \rightarrow 2NaCl + energy$$

   Which of the following statements about the above reaction is true?

   Ⓐ This is an exothermic reaction.

   Ⓑ This is an endothermic reaction.

   Ⓒ Cl atoms are created in this reaction.

   Ⓓ Na atoms are destroyed in this reaction.

Review (cont'd.)

~~~~~~

8. Can two different substances have the same physical property? Explain your answer.

_____

_____

_____

_____

_____

_____

_____

_____

9. A solid is added to water. The temperature of the water rises from 18°C to 22°C. What type of change does this indicate?

_____

_____

_____

_____

_____

_____

_____

_____

Lesson 1   Solubility

The following graph shows the solubility of different solids in water. For example, it shows that at 60°C, 160 grams of sodium chlorate dissolve in 100 mL of water. Use this graph to answer the questions that follow.

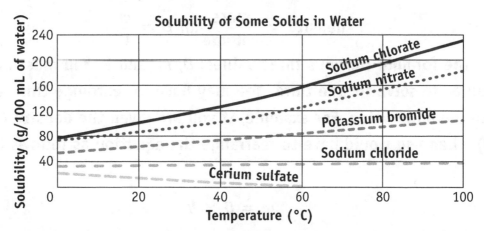

1. Which solid dissolves less as the temperature

   increases? _____

2. How many grams of potassium bromide can dissolve in 100 mL of water at 40°C?

   _____

3. How many grams of sodium chloride can dissolve in 100 mL of water at 80°C?

   _____

4. How many grams of sodium nitrate can dissolve in 200 mL of water at 0°C?

   _____

5. How many grams of sodium chlorate can dissolve in 100 mL of water at 70°C?

   _____

6. At what temperature does cerium sulfate no longer dissolve in water?

   _____

7. Does this graph support the statement that solubility is a physical property that can be used to identify a substance? Explain the reason for your answer.

   _____

   _____

Lesson 1   Density

The following table lists the densities of some common substances. Use the information in this table to answer the questions that follow. Recall that the formula for density is

$$\text{density} = \frac{\text{mass}}{\text{volume}} \text{ or } D = \frac{m}{V}$$

Notice that the formula contains three values: D, m, and V. You must be given two of these values to solve for the third. You may have to rearrange this equation to solve for an unknown value. For example, if you are given the density (D) and volume (V), then you would have to rearrange the equation as follows to solve for mass (m).

$$m = D \times V$$

Densities of Common Substances			
Substance	Density (g/cm^2)	Substance	Density (g/cm^2)
Helium (gas)	0.00001663	Zinc (solid)	7.13
Oxygen (gas)	0.001331	Silver (solid)	10.50
Water (liquid)	1.00	Lead (solid)	11.35
Pyrite (solid)	5.02	Mercury (liquid)	13.55

1. Find the density of a substance that has a mass of 45 grams and a volume of 6.3 cm^3.

_____

2. Based on the above table, what might the substance in question 1 be? _____

3. What is the mass of a sample of pyrite that has a volume of 22 cm^3?

_____

4. Suppose you have a lead ball whose mass is 454 grams. What is the ball's volume?

_____

5. Do these problems support the statement that density is a physical property that can be used to identify a substance? Explain the reason for your answer.

_____

Lesson 1

Chemical Reactions

Use the following list of words to complete each sentence. Each word may be used only once.

reactant	created	destroyed
conservation	equation	exothermic
formula	reactivity	product
endothermic	atoms	

1. A chemical reaction includes a chemical _____ that uses symbols and numbers to represent a substance.

2. During a chemical reaction, mass cannot be either _____ or _____.

3. A reaction that releases energy is known as a(n) _____ reaction.

4. A substance that is made as a result of a chemical reaction is called a(n) _____.

5. A shorthand way to represent a chemical reaction is to use a chemical _____ that includes chemical formulas.

6. A reaction that absorbs energy is known as a(n) _____ reaction.

7. The ability of a substance to undergo a chemical reaction is known as its _____.

8. A(n) _____ is always shown on the left side of the arrow in a chemical equation.

9. As a result of a chemical reaction, the _____ are rearranged.

10. The law that states that atoms are not created or destroyed during a chemical reaction is known

    as the law of _____ of mass.

Lesson 1 — Experiment: Conservation of Mass

You learned that mass is neither created nor destroyed during a chemical reaction. In this experiment, you will carry out a chemical reaction and see what happens to the mass of the reactants.

You Will Need

tablespoon
baking soda
large, sealable plastic bag
film canister
kitchen scale

Procedure

1. Place four tablespoons of baking soda into a large, sealable plastic bag.

2. Fill a plastic film canister with vinegar.

3. Put the lid securely on the canister and carefully place it into the bag.

4. Gently squeeze as much air as possible out of the bag.

5. Seal the bag tightly.

6. Use the kitchen scale to record the weight of the bag and its contents. Note: Although mass and weight are not the same, you can assume that weight represents the mass of the bag and its contents.

7. Keep the bag closed while you remove the lid from the film canister.

8. Mix the baking soda and vinegar.

9. Observe what happens.

10. When the reaction between the baking soda and vinegar has stopped, record the weight of the bag and its contents.

Experiment: Conservation of Mass (cont'd.)

Results and Analysis

1. What indication did you observe that a chemical reaction took place when the baking soda and vinegar were mixed?

_____

_____

_____

_____

_____

_____

2. What was the weight of the bag and its contents before the reaction? _____

3. What was the weight of the bag and its contents after the reaction? _____

Conclusion

What conclusion can you make based on your results?

_____

_____

_____

_____

_____

_____

_____

Lesson 2 Motions and Forces

For thousands of years, people wondered why objects always fell toward Earth. The answer was provided by an English scientist named Isaac Newton (1642–1727). The legend is that Newton discovered the answer after he watched an apple fall from a tree. He concluded that a force made the apple fall. A **force** is a push or pull. In other words, something pulled the apple toward Earth. Newton concluded that the same force kept the planets moving in the orbits around the sun. This force is

gravity. In this lesson, you will learn what Newton discovered about gravity and other factors that affect moving objects, such as a falling apple.

Gravity and Mass

In Lesson 1, you learned that mass is the amount of matter in an object. **Gravity** is the force of attraction between two objects that is due to their masses. Because all objects have mass, then all objects experience an attraction toward all other objects. In other words, an apple falling from a tree is being pulled toward Earth. In turn, Earth is being pulled toward the apple.

Key Terms

force—a push or a pull

gravity—the force of attraction between two objects that is due to their masses

newton—the unit for force

motion—the change in position of an object over time with respect to a reference point

speed—the distance traveled by an object divided by the time taken to travel that distance

inertia—the tendency of an object to resist a change in motion

Newton's first law of motion—the law that states that an object at rest remains at rest and that an object in motion remains in motion at constant speed and in a straight line unless a force causes it to change speed or direction

friction—the force that opposes motion between two surfaces that are in contact

velocity—the speed in a particular direction

acceleration—a change in velocity

Newton's second law of motion—the law that states that the overall force on an object is equal to the mass of the object multiplied by the acceleration of the object

Newton's third law of motion—the law that states that whenever one object exerts a force on a second object, the second object exerts an equal and opposite force on the first object

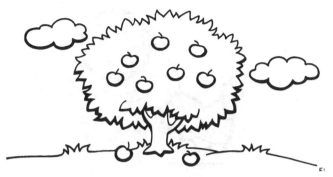

Gravity is a relatively weak force. The mass of an apple is too small to create a force large enough to pull another object toward it. There is one object, however, that has an enormous mass and therefore exerts a force large enough to attract objects.

Earth's Gravity

Compared to every object around, Earth has a huge mass. Because of its mass, Earth exerts a gravitational force on every object. Earth's gravitational force pulls everything toward its center. Because of this force, every object stays in place unless another force is large enough to overcome Earth's gravitational force.

For example, even you can overcome the pull of Earth's enormous gravity by lifting something or jumping off the ground. However, overcoming Earth's gravitational force is only temporary. Shortly after you jump off the ground, Earth's gravitational force pulls you right back down.

Gravity acts across short distances, such as the distance between you and Earth when you jump into the air. Gravity also acts across great distances—even across the universe. In 1665, Newton developed a law that describes the force of gravity between any two objects, no matter their masses or the distance between them.

The Law of Universal Gravitation

Newton wrote an equation to summarize the relationship between mass, distance, and the force of gravity. The unit for the force of gravity is the **newton** (N).

F = the force of gravity
G = a small, constant value (6.67 10^{-11} N · m^2/kg^2)
m_1 and m_2 = masses of the two objects
r = the distance between the objects

$$F = \frac{Gm_1m_2}{r^2}$$

As you can see from the equation, the strength of gravity between two objects depends on their masses and the distance between them. The greater the masses of the objects, the stronger the pull of gravity is. The greater the distance between the objects, the weaker the pull of gravity is.

Gravitational force decreases as a function of the square of the distance. Therefore, gravitational force falls off dramatically as distance increases. Suppose two objects one meter apart have one newton (1N) of gravity between them. If the distance doubles to two meters, the force of gravity between them will be one-fourth of a newton (0.25N). At three meters, it will be one-ninth of a newton (0.11N).

Motion

Did you know that you can tell if an object is moving only by looking at another object at the same time? For example, you know that an apple falling from a tree is moving because it is dropping toward Earth. You see that the apple moves, while Earth stays in place. The object that stays in place is called a reference point.

When an object changes position over time with respect to a reference point, the object is in **motion**. Motion is often described in terms of speed. **Speed** is the distance traveled by an object divided by the time taken to travel that distance. The speed of a car may be 50 miles per hour, which means that the car travels 50 miles in 1 hour. Newton developed three laws to describe the motion of objects.

Newton's First Law of Motion

Objects have a natural tendency to resist a change in motion. If an object is at rest, the object will remain at rest until a force causes the object to move. Also, if an object is in motion, the object will keep on moving in the same direction and at the same speed until a force acts on it to change its direction or speed.

The tendency of an object to resist a change in motion is called **inertia**. Mass is a measure of inertia. The more mass an object has, the greater its inertia. A bowling ball has much more mass, and therefore more inertia, than a soccer ball. This is why it is much harder to get a bowling ball moving. Once the bowling ball is moving, it will also be much harder to stop it than a moving soccer ball.

Newton's first law of motion states that an object at rest remains at rest and that an object in motion remains in motion at constant speed and in a straight line unless a force causes it to change speed or direction. Newton's first law of motion is also known as the law of inertia.

The first part of this law about an object at rest may seem obvious to you. For example, a chair will not slide across the room unless you push it, and a soccer ball will not fly through the air unless you kick it.

The second part of this law makes sense if you think about an object moving with a certain speed. Suppose a pitcher throws a baseball. The ball's speed and direction change when it is hit by a batter or caught by a catcher. Both the batter and catcher provide the force to change the motion of the ball. The batter provided a force that changed the speed and direction of the ball. The catcher provided the force to stop the motion of the ball. However, it is not always so obvious that a force is required to stop an object's motion.

Suppose you slide a box across the floor. According to Newton's first law of motion, the box should move forever unless another force acts on it. What makes the box stop if it does not hit anything and no one stops it? The force that stops the box is friction. **Friction** is a force that opposes motion between two surfaces that are in contact. The friction between the box and the floor opposes the motion of the box.

Newton's Second Law of Motion

Newton's second law of motion deals with acceleration. Recall that speed is distance divided by time. The speed in a particular direction is called **velocity**. For example, the velocity of a car may be 50 miles/hour east. **Acceleration** is a change in velocity. Acceleration occurs when a car speeds up, slows down, or turns.

Newton's second law of motion states that the overall force on an object is equal to the mass of the object multiplied by the acceleration of the object. This law can be expressed mathematically as the following equation.

$$\text{force} = \text{mass} \times \text{acceleration} \text{ or } F = m \times a$$

You can rearrange this equation as follows.

$$\text{acceleration} = \frac{\text{force}}{\text{mass}} \text{ or } a = \frac{F}{m}$$

From the above equation, you can see that acceleration depends on force and mass. An object's acceleration increases as the force on the object increases. In contrast, an object's acceleration decreases as the mass of the object increases.

This makes sense if you think about riding a bicycle. You must exert a force on the pedals of a bicycle to start it moving. If you want to accelerate quickly, you apply as much force as possible by pedaling as hard as you can. However, you would not accelerate as quickly if you applied the same amount of force to a bicycle that has more mass.

Newton's Third Law of Motion

Newton's third law of motion states that whenever one object exerts a force on a second object, the second object exerts an equal and opposite force on the first object.

Newton's third law explains how you can swim through the water. Your hands exert a force on the water. In turn, the water exerts a force on your hands moving you forward. The force your hands exert is called the action force. The force the water exerts is called the reaction force. This is why Newton's third law is also known as the law of action-reaction.

All forces act in action-reaction pairs. Action and reaction forces act on different objects. When you swim, you exert a force on the water, while the water exerts a force on you. When fuel is burned in a rocket, the gases produced are expelled out of the bottom of the rocket. When the gases are forced downward toward the ground, they exert an equal force on the rocket in the upward direction. This force pushes the rocket upward.

Lesson 2   Review

Darken the circle for the best answer.

1. What two factors must be known to calculate the speed of an object in motion?

   Ⓐ direction and type of force being applied

   Ⓑ distance and direction

   Ⓒ distance and type of force being applied

   Ⓓ distance and time

2. Which two factors affect the gravitational attraction between two objects?

   Ⓐ mass and distance

   Ⓑ weight and distance

   Ⓒ size and chemical composition

   Ⓓ mass and weight

3. Alison kicks a soccer ball across the field. What causes the ball to come to a stop?

   Ⓐ It changes direction.

   Ⓑ Its mass increases.

   Ⓒ Gravity acts on it.

   Ⓓ Friction acts on it.

4. How are force, mass, and acceleration related according to Newton's second law of motion?

   Ⓐ mass = force × acceleration

   Ⓑ force = mass × acceleration

   Ⓒ force = mass ÷ acceleration

   Ⓓ acceleration = mass ÷ force

5. Which of the following is associated with inertia?

   Ⓐ Newton's first law of motion

   Ⓑ Newton's second law of motion

   Ⓒ Newton's third law of motion

   Ⓓ action-reaction pair

6. If the distance between two objects is reduced by half, then the gravitation force between them

   Ⓐ increases by a factor of four.

   Ⓑ is reduced by half.

   Ⓒ remains constant.

   Ⓓ increases by a factor of two.

7. Use Newton's first law of motion to explain why airbags in cars are important during a head-on collision.

   _____

   _____

8. Use Newton's second law of motion to explain why it takes less force to accelerate a car than a truck.

   _____

   _____

9. Use Newton's third law of motion to explain why your hand hurts if you bump it hard against the edge of a table.

   _____

   _____

Lesson 2   Motion

The graph below shows the data collected by a student as she watched a squirrel running along the ground. Use this graph to answer the questions that follow.

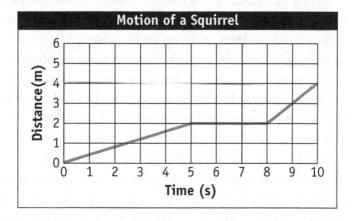

1. What was the average speed of the squirrel during the entire time its motion was observed?

2. What was the average speed of the squirrel between 0 seconds and 5 seconds?

3. What was the average speed of the squirrel between 8 seconds and 10 seconds?

4. Describe the squirrel's motion between 5 seconds and 8 seconds.

_____

5. Describe what the graph would look like if the squirrel moved backward.

_____

_____

Lesson 2

A Roller-Coaster Ride

Read the following passage. Then answer the questions that follow the passage.

It's like a giant roller coaster moving at 35,000 feet above the ground. It moves upward at a steep angle and then turns to fall back down at a 45-degree angle. Then it turns and heads right back up, drops downward again, repeating this up-and-down ride more times than an actual roller coaster.

The giant roller coaster in the sky is a KC-135 airplane that has been modified for NASA. The modifications were made so that NASA can use the plane to train its astronauts for its space shuttle missions. While in orbit above Earth, a space shuttle is always moving forward at a constant speed. If there were no gravity, the shuttle would move straight out into space. But Earth's gravity also attracts the space shuttle. As a result, the shuttle is also moving straight down. The forward and downward motions combine to cause orbiting.

Any object orbiting Earth is in free fall. Free fall is the motion of an object when only the force of gravity is acting on it. Sky divers are said to be in free fall before they open their parachutes. However, there is another force acting on a sky diver falling through the air. This force is air resistance. Astronauts do not encounter air resistance inside a shuttle. So the astronauts inside a shuttle are truly in free fall. Because astronauts are in free fall, they float.

As the KC-135 descends sharply, the people aboard are also in free fall. NASA uses a KC-135 to have people experience what free fall feels like. It's like being weightless.

1. What is the main idea of this passage?

   (A) Traveling aboard a space shuttle is similar to traveling on Earth.

   (B) NASA prepares astronauts for missions in space by having them fly on a KC-135.

   (C) Sky divers and astronauts on the space shuttle experience free fall.

   (D) A KC-135 flies like a giant roller coaster in the sky.

2. What force causes a space shuttle to move straight down?

   (A) air resistance

   (B) rocket thrusters

   (C) gravity

   (D) free fall

3. Which of the following explains why a space shuttle moves forward at a constant speed?

   (A) Newton's first law

   (B) Newton's second law

   (C) gravity

   (D) force = mass × acceleration

4. Although astronauts aboard a space shuttle can float, they are not weightless because they still have

   (A) speed.

   (B) inertia.

   (C) motion.

   (D) mass.

Lesson 2   A Newtonian Crossword Puzzle

Across

5. besides mass, another factor affects force
7. what there must be if there is an action
8. Newton's law that is also called the law of inertia
9. Did Newton really see one falling?
10. force of attraction between two masses
11. Newton's law that states that forces act in pairs
13. Newton's law that states that $F = m \times a$

Down

1. what you must increase to increase acceleration if the mass stays constant
2. unit for force
3. tendency to resist change in motion
4. what happens to the force of gravity as objects get closer
6. speed in a particular direction
8. what makes Newton's first law difficult to see
12. common word for force

Lesson 2   Experiment: Acceleration Due to Gravity

Another legend in science centers on an Italian scientist named Galileo Galilei. According to one story, in the late 1500s, Galileo dropped two cannonballs of different masses from the top of the Leaning Tower of Pisa in Italy. At that time, most people believed that the more mass an object has, the faster it would fall to Earth because of gravity. In this experiment, you will have the opportunity to repeat what Galileo did to check how gravity affects the acceleration of objects. But you will not need cannonballs to do it.

You Will Need

string
high place such as a second-story window to serve as a drop point
measuring tape
someone to help you
golf ball
stopwatch
softball
basketball

Procedure

1. Hang a string from your drop point so that it touches the ground.

2. Cut the string and measure its length. This represents the distance the objects will travel as they drop to the ground.

3. Have someone hold the golf ball from the drop point.

4. Say "Drop" and start the stopwatch at exactly the same time.

5. Time how long it takes the golf ball to reach the ground.

6. Repeat steps 3–5 four more times.

7. Repeat steps 3–5 five times, using a softball.

Experiment: Acceleration Due to Gravity (cont'd.)

8. Repeat steps 3–5 five times, using a basketball.

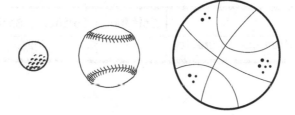

Results and Analysis

1. Organize your data in a table.

	Golf ball	Softball	Basketball
Trial 1			
Trial 2			
Trial 3			
Trial 4			
Trial 5			
Average time			

2. Calculate the acceleration of each ball you dropped. The following is the equation for acceleration. Use your average time for each ball.

$$\text{acceleration} = \frac{\text{final velocity minus starting velocity}}{\text{time it takes to change velocity}}$$

Velocity is calculated as follows.

$$\text{velocity} = \frac{\text{distance traveled}}{\text{time taken}}$$

Assume that a ball takes 2 seconds to fall 120 feet. Its final velocity is 120 feet/2 seconds or 60 feet/second downward. Its initial velocity was zero because the ball was not moving. Therefore, the acceleration of the ball is calculated as follows.

$$\text{acceleration} = \frac{60 \text{ feet/second} - 0 \text{ feet/second}}{2 \text{ seconds}} = 30 \text{ feet/second squared (f/s}^2)$$

Experiment: Acceleration Due to Gravity (cont'd.)

Organize your data in a table.

	Golf ball	Softball	Basketball
Acceleration due to gravity			

Conclusions

1. What conclusion can you draw from your data?

_____

_____

_____

_____

_____

2. Acceleration due to gravity is 32 f/s^2 or 9.8 m/s^2. How do your results compare to this value?

_____

_____

_____

_____

3. What might have caused your results to differ from the actual value?

_____

_____

_____

_____

Lesson 3 Transfer of Energy

In Lesson 1, you learned that chemical reactions obey the law of conservation of mass. Recall that the atoms in the reactants are simply rearranged to form the products. You also learned that energy is involved. Exothermic reactions release energy. Endothermic reactions absorb energy. In this lesson, you will take a closer look at what happens to energy during chemical reactions. You will also learn what happens to energy during nuclear reactions.

Energy

If you ask ten people what energy is, you are likely to get ten different answers. In science, however, energy has just one meaning. **Energy** is the ability to do work. For example, you use energy to turn the pages of a book, a radio uses energy to make sounds, and a solar-powered calculator uses energy to function. There are different forms of energy. You depend on chemical energy to turn the pages. A radio uses electrical energy to make sounds. A calculator uses light energy to function.

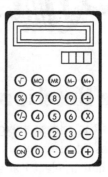

energy—the ability to do work

activation energy—the smallest amount of energy required to start a chemical reaction

law of conservation of energy—the law that states that energy cannot be either created or destroyed

chemical energy—the energy of a substance that changes as its atoms are rearranged

proton—a particle that makes up part of the nucleus of an atom

neutron—a particle that makes up part of the nucleus of an atom

nucleus—the central part of an atom

electron—a particle that orbits the nucleus of an atom

nuclear reaction—a reaction involving the nucleus of an atom

nuclear fission—the process by which a nucleus splits into two smaller nuclei, releasing a tremendous amount of energy

nuclear chain reaction—a continuous series of nuclear reactions

nuclear fusion—the process by which two smaller atomic nuclei combine to form a larger nucleus, releasing a tremendous amount of energy

Activation Energy

Have you ever needed a boost of energy to start working? Chemical reactions also need a boost of energy to get started. This boost of energy is called the activation energy. The **activation energy** is the smallest amount of energy required to start a chemical reaction.

For some reactions, the activation energy is fairly small. If you drop a piece of sodium metal in water, an explosive reaction occurs. This reaction requires very little activation energy. Other reactions require more activation energy. Spark plugs must be ignited to start the burning of gasoline in a car's engine.

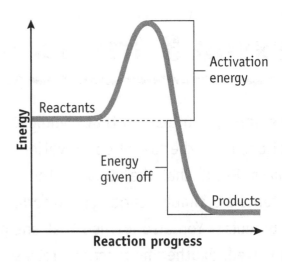

The above graph shows that the reactants have a certain amount of chemical energy. However, additional energy is needed before the reaction can take place. This additional energy is the activation energy. Notice that when the reaction is completed, the chemical energy of the products is less than the chemical energy of the reactants. This means that energy has been released.

Exothermic Reactions

Exothermic reactions can release energy in several forms. Some reactions release energy as heat, others as light, and still others as electrical energy. The energy released in an exothermic reaction is sometimes shown as a product in the equation. Examine the equation that shows the reaction between carbon and oxygen to form carbon dioxide.

$$C + O_2 \rightarrow CO_2 + energy$$

Notice that this is an exothermic reaction because energy is released. Energy is shown as a product in this reaction. One way to analyze the energy change during a chemical reaction is to use an energy diagram. Energy diagrams trace the change in energy during a chemical reaction. Examine the following energy diagram for an exothermic reaction.

Endothermic Reactions

Endothermic reactions can absorb energy in several forms. Some reactions absorb energy as heat, others as light, and still others as electrical energy. The energy absorbed in an endothermic reaction is sometimes shown as a reactant in the equation. Examine the chemical equation that shows what happens when ultraviolet light from the sun strikes the ozone layer in the upper atmosphere.

$$O_3 + energy \rightarrow O_2 + O$$

Notice that this is an endothermic reaction because energy is absorbed. Energy is shown as a reactant in this reaction. The following is an energy diagram for an endothermic reaction.

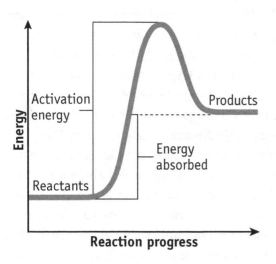

The above graph shows that the reactants have a certain amount of chemical energy. However, additional energy is needed before the reaction can take place. This additional energy is the activation energy. Notice that when the endothermic reaction is complete, the chemical energy of the products is more than the chemical energy of the reactants.

Law of Conservation of Energy

Exothermic reactions do not create the energy they release. Similarly, endothermic reactions do not destroy the energy they absorb. Energy cannot be either created or destroyed. This is known as the **law of conservation of energy**.

The energy released in an exothermic reaction comes from the reactants. Reactants contain a form of energy called chemical energy. **Chemical energy** is the energy of a substance that changes as its atoms are rearranged. During an exothermic reaction, some of the chemical energy in the reactants is changed into the energy that is released. Therefore, the types of energy may change. But the total amount of energy of all types is the same before and after the exothermic reaction.

The energy absorbed during a chemical reaction comes from an external energy source. Take another look at the endothermic reaction you just examined.

$$O_3 + energy \rightarrow O_2 + O$$

Ultraviolet light from the sun provides the energy for this reaction. Some of the ultraviolet energy is changed into the chemical energy found in the products. As a result, the products have more chemical energy than the reactant. Therefore, the types of energy may change. But the total amount of energy of all types is the same before and after the endothermic reaction.

Nuclear Reactions

In the late 1800s, scientists first discovered that an atom could be broken down into smaller particles. They eventually discovered three smaller particles. These are the proton, neutron, and electron. **Protons** and **neutrons** make up the **nucleus**, which is the central part of an atom. **Electrons** orbit the nucleus.

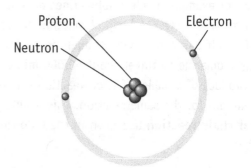

Recall that chemical reactions involve the rearrangement of atoms. Electrons are the particles that take part in chemical reactions. However, the protons and neutrons in the nucleus can also react. When they do, the result is called a **nuclear reaction.** There are two types of nuclear reactions. Both types involve a tremendous amount of energy.

Nuclear Fission

The nucleus of an atom can be unstable. If it is, the nucleus will decay and break into two smaller, more stable nuclei. This process is called **nuclear fission**. As a result of nuclear fission, a tremendous amount of energy is released.

When an unstable nucleus undergoes fission, the total mass of the products is slightly less than the total mass of the reactants. In Lesson 1, you read about the law of conservation of mass. Nuclear fission seems to contradict this law. It does. In nuclear fission, some of the mass of the reactants is converted into energy. Therefore, there is a loss of mass. But the amount of mass that is lost is extremely small. How can this extremely small amount of mass produce an enormous amount of energy?

In 1905, a scientist named Albert Einstein explained how this is possible. That year, Einstein published a paper in which he said that matter can be changed into energy, and vice versa. This relationship is expressed by the equation $E = mc^2$. E represents energy. M represents mass. C represents the speed of light.

The speed of light is 186,000 miles per second. Notice that the speed of light is squared in Einstein's equation. Therefore, an extremely small amount of mass can be converted to an enormous amount of energy. For example, nuclear submarines depend on fission for their power. A lump of material about the size of a golf ball can provide enough power for a nuclear submarine to travel about 60,000 miles.

A product of a nuclear fission reaction can serve as a reactant for the same reaction. This results in a **nuclear chain reaction** as shown in the following illustration.

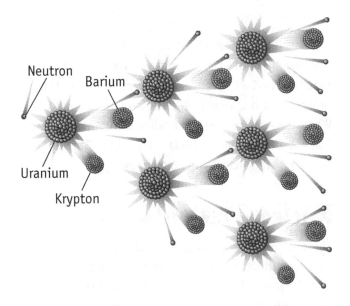

Notice in the illustration that a neutron bombards an atom of uranium. The uranium atom undergoes fission to form three products. These products include a barium atom, a krypton atom, and neutrons. These neutrons can then bombard other uranium atoms, which then undergo fission. The process continues as an uncontrolled nuclear chain reaction. The tremendous energy released by an atomic bomb is the result of an uncontrolled nuclear chain reaction.

On the other hand, nuclear power plants use controlled nuclear chain reactions to release energy. This energy is used to generate electricity. Nuclear power plants reduce our dependence on fossil fuels, such as coal and oil. However, these plants produce nuclear wastes that remain radioactive for thousands of years. In addition, an accident at a nuclear power plant can release radioactive material into the atmosphere. Such an accident occurred in Chernobyl, Ukraine, in 1986.

Nuclear Fusion

Scientists are researching the possibility of using another type of nuclear reaction to use in power plants. This is nuclear fusion. **Nuclear fusion** is the process in which the nuclei of smaller atoms are combined to form one larger nucleus. Like fission, fusion releases a tremendous amount of energy. Fusion is the process by which the sun creates its energy.

Fusion has several advantages over fission. The products of fusion reactions are not radioactive. If a nuclear fusion reactor exploded, very little radioactive material would be released. Unlike uranium, the fuel for a fusion reactor is readily available.

So far, scientists have been able to create a fusion reaction only by supplying more energy than is generated. Aware of the benefits of fusion, scientists are trying to find ways to have a fusion reaction generate more energy than it consumes.

Lesson 3   Review

Darken the circle for the best answer.

1. The energy needed to start a reaction is known as
   - (A) chemical energy.
   - (B) activation energy.
   - (C) nuclear energy.
   - (D) chain reaction.

2. Which of the following statements is true regarding an endothermic reaction?
   - (A) No energy is required to start the reaction.
   - (B) The products contain less energy than the reactants.
   - (C) The products contain more energy than the reactants.
   - (D) Energy is released.

3. Which of the following statements obeys the law of conservation of energy?
   - (A) Energy can be created in a chemical reaction.
   - (B) Energy can be destroyed in a chemical reaction.
   - (C) Nuclear reactions can create energy from mass.
   - (D) Energy can be converted from one form to another.

4. In the equation $E = mc^2$, m represents
   - (A) mass.
   - (B) the speed of light.
   - (C) motion.
   - (D) energy.

5. Which atomic particles can be involved in a nuclear reaction?
   - (A) protons and electrons
   - (B) neutrons and electrons
   - (C) protons and neutrons
   - (D) protons, neutrons, and electrons

6. Examine the following chemical reaction.

   sugar + oxygen → carbon dioxide + water + energy

   Which of the following statements about the above reaction is true?
   - (A) This is an example of an endothermic reaction.
   - (B) The products have less energy than the reactants.
   - (C) This is an example of nuclear fission.
   - (D) The reactants have less energy than the products.

7. Energy is released when smaller nuclei join to form a larger nucleus in a process called

Ⓐ a nuclear chain reaction.

Ⓑ fission.

Ⓒ fusion.

Ⓓ nucleation.

8. How are fusion and fission reactions similar?

_____

_____

_____

_____

_____

_____

_____

9. How are exothermic and endothermic reactions similar?

_____

_____

_____

_____

_____

_____

_____

Lesson 3   Chemical Reactions and Energy I

Examine the following graph, which illustrates the energy changes that occur during a chemical reaction. Use the graph to answer the questions.

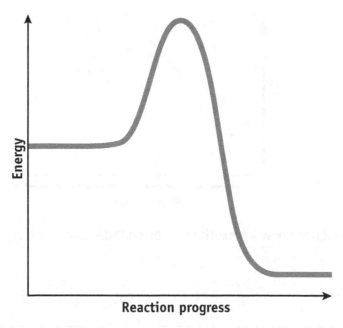

1. Does this energy diagram show an exothermic or endothermic reaction? Explain the reason for your answer.

   _____

   _____

   _____

2. Draw a dashed line on the graph and label it X to show the activation energy.

3. Draw another dashed line on the graph and label it Y to show the energy that is released or absorbed by this reaction.

4. A catalyst is often added to a chemical reaction. A catalyst is a substance that speeds up the rate of a reaction by lowering the activation energy. Draw a third dashed line to show what the above graph will look like if a catalyst is added.

Lesson 3   Chemical Reactions and Energy II

Examine the following graph, which illustrates the energy changes that occur during a chemical reaction. Use the graph to answer the questions.

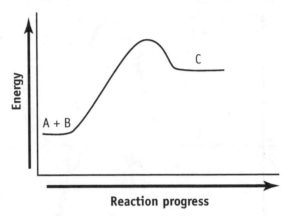

1. Does this energy diagram show an exothermic or endothermic reaction? Explain the reason for your answer.

   _____

   _____

   _____

2. What do A and B represent?

   _____

3. What does C represent?

   _____

4. Draw a dashed line on the graph and label it Y to show the energy that is released or absorbed by this reaction.

Lesson 3   A Long Voyage

Read the following passage and then answer the questions.

Concerns about nuclear accidents have even affected operations carried out by NASA. To study distant objects in our solar system such as Saturn and Pluto, NASA has launched unmanned space probes. A space probe takes about seven years to reach Saturn and nine years to travel to Pluto. The electrical energy needed for such long flights is provided by special devices called radioisotope thermoelectric generators (RTGs).

RTGs use the decay of radioactive materials to generate electricity. The decay actually generates heat, which is then converted to electricity. The space probes use a radioactive material called plutonium-238. This material cannot be used to make nuclear weapons, and therefore it is not considered a target for terrorists. In addition, the plutonium is not placed inside the RTGs in pure form. Rather, the plutonium is installed in ceramic bricks. If an accident occurred, the bricks would shatter into large pieces and not into dust, which is more dangerous.

Although the plutonium is radioactive, the form of radiation it emits is similar to the radiation given off by home smoke detectors. This form of radiation cannot even penetrate a sheet of paper. The only way the radiation can be harmful to humans is to inhale or ingest it. Because the plutonium cannot produce dust particles, the radioactive material is not likely to find its way into humans.

Most NASA missions use solar panels to generate power. They are cheaper and lighter than the RTGs. Then why doesn't NASA use solar panels on space probes heading out to the distant planets? If NASA used solar panels, they would have to be many times larger because the sunlight is much dimmer in distant space. In fact, the solar panels would be so large that they would cover one-fourth of a football field. Panels that large would be impossible to control.

1. Why is the plutonium used in RTGs not considered a terrorist target?

_____

2. Why is the plutonium assembled into ceramic bricks?

_____

_____

3. What are the energy conversions that occur in an RTG?

_____

4. What do smoke detectors have in common with RTGs?

_____

Lesson 3 — Experiment: A Model of Nuclear Fission

Scientists often use models to simulate the real world. These models can be quite sophisticated, especially if a computer is used. However, scientific models can be quite simple. For example, you will use pennies to simulate what happens when a radioactive substance decays or undergoes fission. All radioactive substances decay in a predictable manner. Each substance has a certain half-life. A half-life is the amount of time it takes for one-half of a radioactive substance to decay. If you have 4 ounces of a radioactive substance, then only 2 ounces will remain after one half-life. After another half-life, only 1 ounce will remain, and so on. In this experiment, pennies can serve as models to demonstrate the concept of half-life.

You Will Need

200 pennies
plastic container with lid
clock or watch with second hand
graph paper
ruler
pencil

Procedure

1. Place the pennies in the container and cover tightly.

2. Shake the pennies by repeatedly turning the container upside down and back up for 10 seconds.

3. Open the container and spill the pennies on a flat surface.

4. Remove all the pennies that are tails up.

5. Count the number of pennies that are left and place them back in the container.

6. Repeat steps 2–5 until there are no pennies left to place back in the container.

Experiment: A Model of Nuclear Fission (cont'd.)

7. Make a graph of your results. Plot the number of times you carried out steps 2–6 along the horizontal axis. Plot the number of pennies that landed hands up each time along the vertical axis.

Results and Analysis

1. How many pennies are removed after each shake?

_____

2. What is the half-life of your "radioactive" substance (the pennies)?

_____

Conclusion

What conclusion can you draw based on your results?

_____

_____

_____

_____

_____

_____

_____

_____

_____

_____

_____

_____

Lesson 4 Structure and Function in Living Systems

All living things, or **organisms**, are made of cells. A **cell** is the smallest unit of an organism that can perform all life processes. Similar cells work together to form a **tissue**. For example, muscle cells make up muscle tissue. Two or more tissues work together to form an **organ**. For example, muscle tissue and nervous tissue make up the stomach. Organs that work together make up an **organ system**. For example, the stomach works with other organs to make up the digestive system. Organisms, such as humans, contain several organ systems that all work together to carry out life processes and maintain good health.

Key Terms

organism—a living thing

cell—the smallest unit of an organism that can perform all life processes

tissue—a group of cells that work together for a specific job

organ—a group of tissues that work together for a specific job

organ system—a group of organs that work together for a specific job

kidney—the organ that filters wastes from the blood and produces urine

nephron—the unit in the kidney that filters blood

ureter—the tube that connects the kidney to the urinary bladder

urethra—the tube that leads from the urinary bladder to the outside of the body

testis—the male reproductive organ where sperm are produced

ovary—the female reproductive organ where eggs are produced

fallopian tube—a tube that leads from the ovary to the uterus

uterus—the site where a fertilized egg develops into a fetus

menstrual cycle—the 28-day cycle that involves changes in the female reproductive system

endocrine system—the system that controls body functions by using chemicals

hormone—a substance made in one cell or tissue that causes a change in another cell or tissue

central nervous system—the brain and spinal cord

peripheral nervous system—the parts of the nervous system other than the brain and spinal cord

cerebrum—the part of the brain that gathers, interprets, and responds to information

cerebellum—the part of the brain that controls muscle coordination

medulla—the part of the brain that controls involuntary processes

reflex—an involuntary response that does not involve the brain

Excretory System

The main organ of the excretory system is the kidney. There are two kidneys in the human body. The **kidneys** remove waste products from the blood. The wastes that are removed from the blood are converted into urine.

Each day, the kidneys filter about 520 gallons of blood. The human body contains about 1.5 gallons of blood. Therefore, the blood cycles through the kidneys about 350 times a day, or about 15 times every hour. Each day, the kidneys produce between 3 cups and 2 quarts of urine. The volume of urine produced depends on several factors, especially the volume of liquids that a person drinks.

Each kidney is made up of tiny filters called **nephrons**. There are more than 1 million nephrons in each kidney. The urine that is produced by all these nephrons passes into a tube called the **ureter**. A ureter from each kidney empties into the urinary bladder where the urine is stored. The urine is eliminated through another tube called the **urethra**.

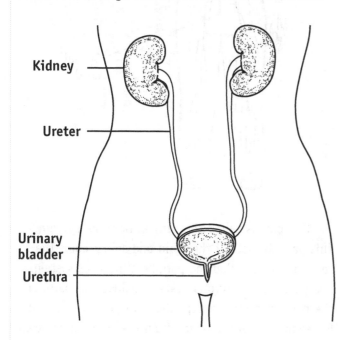

Reproductive System

The male reproductive system produces sperm. Sperm are matured in the **testes** and pass out the body through the urethra in the penis. The female reproductive system produces eggs. Eggs are formed in the **ovaries**. An egg travels from the ovary to a fallopian tube. A **fallopian tube** from each ovary leads to the uterus. The **uterus** is the organ in which a fetus will develop.

The formation of an egg in the ovary is a complex process that spans about 28 days. This period of time is called a **menstrual cycle**. During this cycle, several chemical substances known as hormones are produced. These hormones prepare the egg for fertilization by a sperm. These hormones also prepare the uterus should fertilization occur. The uterus becomes thicker and contains more blood vessels. If fertilization occurs, then the uterus is prepared so that the fetus can develop for the next nine months. Several structures, including the placenta and umbilical cord, serve as the life support system for the developing fetus.

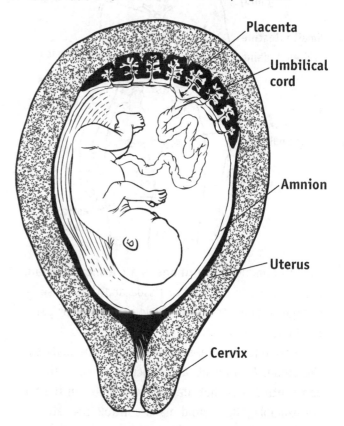

If fertilization does not occur, then the uterine lining is shed. The menstrual cycle starts again.

In the United States, about 15 percent of married couples cannot have a child. Many of these couples are infertile, which means that their reproductive systems are not functioning properly. The men may not be able to produce sperm. The women may not be able to produce eggs. Sexually transmitted diseases such as gonorrhea can lead to infertility in women. These diseases can also cause infertility in men, but not as commonly as they do in women.

The Endocrine System

The hormones involved in reproduction are part of the endocrine system. The **endocrine system** controls body function by using chemicals. These chemicals are

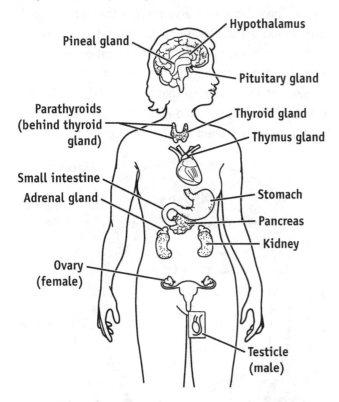

called hormones. A **hormone** is a chemical substance that is made in one cell or tissue and that causes a change in another cell or tissue in a different part of the body.

Hormones are transported through the body by the blood. As a result, an endocrine gland in the neck can control cells that are somewhere else in the body. For example, the thyroid gland controls the rate at which cells throughout the body use sugar for energy.

As the illustration above shows, the endocrine glands are located throughout the body. Notice that

some organs of the endocrine system are also part of other systems. For example, the ovaries are part of both the reproductive and endocrine systems.

Nervous System

Your nervous system receives and sends electrical messages throughout your body. It gathers information from both inside and outside your body. It then interprets this information. Finally, the nervous system responds to that information as needed. To perform these functions, the nervous system has two parts.

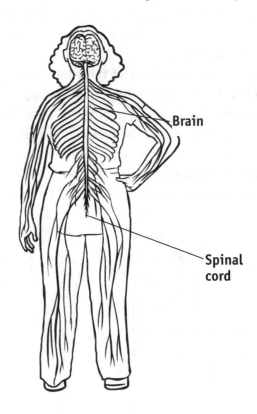

One part is called the **central nervous system**. This part consists of the brain and spinal cord. The second part is called the peripheral nervous system. The **peripheral nervous system** includes all parts of the nervous system except the brain and spinal cord. For example, nerves extend from the spinal cord down the length of the arm. These nerves are part of the peripheral nervous system.

The largest part of the brain is the cerebrum. The **cerebrum** plays a major role in processing information and coordinating responses. For example, the cerebrum interprets sounds and directs your attention to their source. The cerebrum is also where

www.harcourtschoolsupply.com
42
Lesson 4, Structure and Function in Living Systems
Science 8, SV 9781419034367

you think and store memories. Just below the cerebrum is the **cerebellum**, which coordinates muscle action. The cerebellum allows you to regain your balance if you trip and stumble. At the base of the brain is the medulla, which connects to the spinal cord. The **medulla** controls involuntary processes, such as body temperature and blood pressure.

The body sometimes responds to information without involving the brain. For example, you automatically pull away your foot if you step on a sharp object. Reactions that do not involve the brain are called **reflexes**.

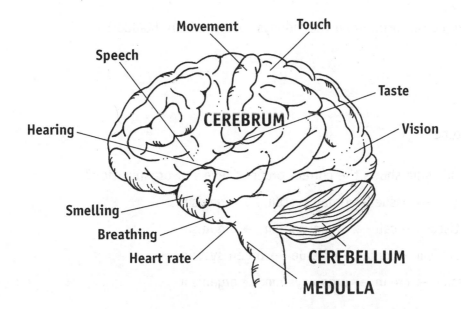

Lesson 4 Review

Darken the circle for the best answer.

1. Which structure carries urine from the kidneys to the urinary bladder?

Ⓐ urethra

Ⓑ ureter

Ⓒ nephron

Ⓓ fallopian tube

2. Which of the following shows the correct order of levels of organization?

Ⓐ cell → organ → tissue → organ system → organism

Ⓑ organ → tissue → cell → organ system → organism

Ⓒ cell → organism → organ → tissue → organ system

Ⓓ cell → tissue → organ → organ system → organism

3. Which event occurs during the menstrual cycle?

Ⓐ A sperm fertilizes an egg.

Ⓑ Sperm are produced in the testes.

Ⓒ Hormones prepare the uterus should fertilization occur.

Ⓓ An egg travels up the fallopian tube to an ovary.

4. Which of the following terms are <u>not</u> correctly paired?

Ⓐ cerebrum—memory storage

Ⓑ cerebellum—muscle coordination

Ⓒ medulla—thinking

Ⓓ central nervous system—brain and spinal cord

5. Which of the following systems is correctly paired with the function it performs?

Ⓐ excretory system—filters the blood

Ⓑ endocrine system—produces urine

Ⓒ nervous system—matures sperm and eggs

Ⓓ reproductive system—controls involuntary responses

Review (cont'd.)

~~~~~~

6. Can one organ function as part of two different body systems? Explain your answer.

_____

_____

_____

_____

_____

7. Which part of the brain is most highly developed in humans compared to other animals? Explain the reason for your choice.

_____

_____

_____

_____

_____

8. How is it possible for the pituitary, which is an endocrine gland in the brain, to control the development of eggs in the ovary?

_____

_____

_____

_____

_____

Lesson 4

When the Kidneys Don't Work

Read the following passage and then answer the questions.

Damage to the nephrons can prevent the kidneys from functioning normally. This damage can be caused by severe, uncontrollable high blood pressure. Infections and diabetes can also result in damage to nephrons. The damage may reduce the kidneys' abilities to filter the blood. In this case, a device called a dialysis machine can be used to filter the blood. The blood from the person passes through special tubing in this machine. As the blood flows through the tubing, wastes are removed. The wastes collect in the machine. The purified blood then flows back to the person. This cycle is repeated until the blood has been essentially cleaned of its wastes.

A dialysis machine, however, cannot help a person whose kidneys have totally stopped functioning. In this case, a kidney transplant may be performed. The first successful kidney transplants were performed with animals in 1902 in Austria. In 1909, French doctors transplanted slices of rabbit kidney into a child. Unfortunately, the child died about two weeks later because this procedure did not produce a functioning kidney. The first successful human-to-human kidney transplant was performed in 1954. The procedure was performed between identical twins in a Boston hospital.

When Richard Herrick, one of the twins, arrived at the hospital, he did not have much time to live because his kidneys were not functioning. His twin brother, Robert, donated one of his kidneys, and it was transplanted into Richard. The operation was a success, and Richard recovered. He married and had two children. Unfortunately, Richard died 8 years later when his transplanted kidney suddenly stopped functioning. In 2004, Robert returned to the hospital to celebrate the fiftieth anniversary of this first successful human kidney transplant.

1. How does a dialysis machine operate?

_____

_____

_____

_____

_____

_____

2. Over 9000 kidney transplants are performed each year in the United States. Under what conditions is a kidney transplant necessary?

_____

_____

_____

_____

_____

_____

3. Can a person live a normal life with just one kidney? Explain.

_____

_____

_____

_____

_____

Lesson 4   Hormones and Reproduction

The following graph illustrates the cycles of the female hormone estrogen and the male hormone testosterone over a period of 28 days. Use the graph below to answer the questions that follow.

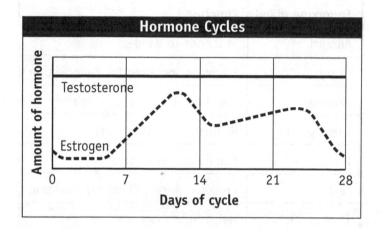

1. What is the major difference between the levels of the two hormones over the 28 days?

_____

_____

2. What might estrogen be doing between days 7 and 12 as its level increases?

_____

_____

3. Why might the level of testosterone remain the same?

_____

_____

4. Do you think that the estrogen levels would change the same way in a pregnant woman? Explain your answer.

_____

_____

Lesson 4   The Endocrine System

The following table lists several endocrine glands and their functions. Answer the questions below based on the information in this table.

Endocrine gland	Function
Adrenal	Responds to danger
Ovary	Produces hormones for reproduction
Pancreas	Regulates blood sugar levels
Parathyroid	Regulates calcium levels
Pineal	Regulates sleep patterns
Testis	Produces hormones for reproduction
Thymus	Helps fight disease
Thyroid	Controls rate of energy use

1. Can a person who is having trouble sleeping have a problem with his or her endocrine system? Explain your answer.

_____

_____

2. Which endocrine gland becomes active if you are suddenly startled by a loud noise?

_____

3. Cells use sugar for their energy needs. Which endocrine glands are involved in helping cells meet their energy needs?

_____

4. How does the endocrine system differ between males and females?

_____

_____

5. The hormone glucagon is released when the sugar level in the blood falls below normal. Which endocrine gland produces glucagon?

_____

6. If an infection occurs, which endocrine gland helps protect the body?

_____

Lesson 4   Experiment: The Nervous System

Nerves extend out from the spinal cord to all parts of the body. Some of these nerves send tiny branches to the skin. These nerves constantly receive information that they send to the brain for interpretation and appropriate action. Some of the information they receive involves temperature, pressure, and pain. In this experiment, you will produce a map of the back of your hand that shows the locations of the nerve cells that detect these sensations.

You Will Need

an assistant
washable fine point marker
ruler
plain paper
eyedropper
cup
sewing needle
water
paper towel

Procedure

1. Use the marker to make a $1\frac{1}{2}$ inch $\times$ $1\frac{1}{2}$ inch square on the back of your hand. Mark off points $\frac{1}{4}$ inch apart along each side of the square. Use a ruler to make a grid by connecting the points with lines. You should have 36 squares, each measuring $\frac{1}{4}$ inch $\times$ $\frac{1}{4}$ inch, in the grid.

2. Use the marker to make three separate grids on paper. Each grid should have the same dimensions as the one on the back of your hand. Label one grid "Cold," the second grid "Hot," and the third grid "Pressure."

3. Turn away while your assistant uses the eyedropper to apply one drop of cold water to each square on the grid on your hand. Have your assistant mark an X on the "cold" grid to show where you felt the cold water. Your assistant should use a paper towel to blot the drop of water as soon as the information has been recorded on the paper.

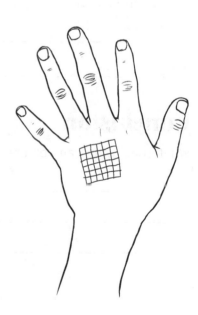

Experiment: The Nervous System (cont'd.)

4. Repeat step 3 using hot water. Be careful that the water is not too hot.

5. Repeat step 3 using the <u>blunt</u> end of the needle to test for pressure. Your assistant should use a light touch.

Results and Analysis

1. Count the number of areas on the back of your hand that were sensitive to cold water. Do the same for hot water and pressure. Does the back of your hand contain nerves that detect one sensation more than the others?

_____

_____

2. Are there areas on the back of your hand that respond to both heat and pressure?

_____

_____

3. Do you think that you would get the same results if you tested an identical area on your leg? Explain your answer.

_____

_____

Conclusion

What conclusion can you draw based on your results?

_____

_____

_____

Lesson 5 Reproduction and Heredity

All organisms reproduce, or make more organisms that are similar to themselves. Reproduction also involves the passing of traits from parents to offspring. The passing of traits from parents to offspring is called **heredity**. Heredity is controlled by genes. A **gene** is a set of instructions for an inherited trait. For example, a gene may contain the instructions that determine the color of a person's eyes. The genes are located on structures inside a cell called **chromosomes**. After scientists recognized that chromosomes store the genetic information, they began an intensive search to learn more about the structure and chemical composition of chromosomes.

Chromosomes and DNA

Chromosomes are made from a chemical compound called **deoxyribonucleic acid**, abbreviated as **DNA**. The genes that are passed from one generation to the next are made of DNA. Knowing the structure of DNA would help scientists understand how DNA functions to control the development of traits in an individual. This is exactly what James Watson and Francis Crick were trying to do in the early 1950s.

Watson and Crick used data that other scientists had obtained about the chemical composition of DNA. For example, scientists knew that DNA consisted of four chemical compounds called bases. These four bases include adenine, thymine, cytosine, and guanine. Scientists had also discovered that the

amount of thymine (T) always equals the amount of adenine (A) in DNA. They also knew that the amount of cytosine (C) always equals the amount of guanine (G) in DNA. Put simply, they knew that A = T and that G = C.

Scientists also knew that DNA contained a sugar called deoxyribose and another chemical compound called phosphate. But just how were the four bases,

Key Terms

heredity—the passing of traits from parents to offspring

gene—a set of instructions stored on a chromosome that determines a particular trait

chromosome—the cell structure that stores the hereditary information

deoxyribonucleic acid (DNA)—the chemical substance in a chromosome that contains the hereditary information

ribonucleic acid (RNA)—the chemical substance that plays a role in the production of proteins

mutation—a change in a gene or DNA

genetic engineering—the manipulation of genes for practical purposes

recombinant DNA—the combination of DNA from two or more sources

genome—the complete set of an organism's DNA

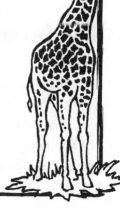

deoxyribose sugars, and phosphates arranged to form the structure of DNA? Watson and Crick used models to answer this question.

The Four Parts of DNA

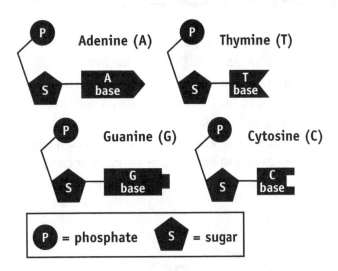

Scientific Models
=================

Making models is one way scientists try to understand the natural world, including the structure of chemical substances such as DNA. Watson and Crick built their DNA model from wire and paper, using the information that other scientists had gathered.

In 1953, Watson and Crick published their results in a scientific paper showing how these data fit their model. In 1962, Watson and Crick were awarded a Nobel Prize, the highest recognition a scientist can achieve. In a book Watson later published, he recounted how photographs taken by another scientist named Rosalind Franklin were critical to their work. Franklin never shared in the glory for her contribution. In 1958, she died from cancer at the age of 37.

The Double Helix
================

The structure of DNA is known as a *double helix*. Think of a double helix as a ladder that is twisted to form a spiral. Like a ladder, DNA can be thought of as having two sides and a series of steps. The two sides of DNA are made form the deoxyribose sugars and phosphates. The steps of the ladder are made from the bases.

One base is joined to each side. For example, the base T may be joined to one side. According to the model built by Watson and Crick, the opposite side of the ladder would have the base A. If one side contained the base G, then the opposite side must have the base C. Two bases, either an A-T pair or a G-C pair, form the steps of the DNA double helix.

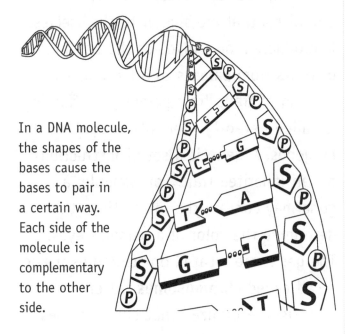

In a DNA molecule, the shapes of the bases cause the bases to pair in a certain way. Each side of the molecule is complementary to the other side.

DNA, RNA, and Proteins
======================

The hereditary information contained in DNA is transferred to another molecule called **ribonucleic acid**, abbreviated as **RNA**. RNA directs how proteins will be assembled. Proteins are chemical substances that play a major role in an organism. Some proteins are used to build cells. Other proteins control the chemical reactions that take place inside the cells. In effect, proteins determine the traits that an individual possesses. For example, proteins help determine how tall you grow, the color of your eyes, and whether your hair is straight or curly. The flow of genetic information can be summarized as follows.

$$DNA \rightarrow RNA \rightarrow protein \rightarrow trait$$

Mutations
=========

If you again look at how genetic information flows from DNA to the development of a trait, you will see that if any change is made in DNA, then this will result in a change in RNA. In turn, a change in RNA can result in a change in a protein. Changing the protein can result in a change in a trait.

Any change in DNA is called a **mutation**. Mutations occur spontaneously. Mutations are also caused by environmental factors, such as ultraviolet light and certain chemicals.

Mutations can occur at several points along the flow of genetic information from DNA to a trait. A mutation can occur when DNA transfers the genetic information to RNA. Mutations can also occur when the protein is being assembled.

The impact of mutations varies widely. Some mutations may have no effect on an organism or its offspring. Other mutations are lethal and can cause death often before birth. Still other mutations can result in disorders that may be minor or life-threatening.

An example of a mutation that is life-threatening is a disease called sickle cell anemia. This disease is characterized by abnormally shaped red blood cells. These blood cells cannot carry enough oxygen to the cells in a person with sickle cell anemia. Without sufficient oxygen, the brain, heart, and many other organs may suffer damage.

Red blood cells contain a protein called hemoglobin that carries oxygen. People with sickle cell anemia have an abnormal form of hemoglobin, which cannot carry as much oxygen. This abnormal hemoglobin is the result of a change in just one base in the DNA of the people with this disease. Changing one base in the DNA causes a change in the RNA that is made. In turn, the change in RNA brings about a change in the hemoglobin that is made.

Genetic Engineering

For hundreds of years, people have been raising plants and animals with the traits they find desirable. Organisms with preferred traits are selected for crosses that have produced a variety of crop plants and domesticated animals. Breeders have successfully developed organisms that are larger, provide more food, or are resistant to certain diseases. Today, scientists have developed new techniques that involve manipulating genes to create organisms with desirable traits.

The manipulation of genes for practical purposes is known as **genetic engineering**. Genetic engineering can be used to cure diseases, treat genetic disorders, create inexpensive ways of making huge quantities of valuable drugs, and do many other things that can improve the lives of humans. Genetic engineering is also used to take a gene from one organism and splice it into the DNA of another organism. The combination of DNA from two or more sources is called **recombinant DNA**. For example, scientists have taken the human gene for insulin and spliced it into the DNA of bacteria.

Insulin is used by diabetics to control their blood sugar level. At one time, the insulin was obtained from processing the organs from animals. Today, genetic engineering has produced bacteria that manufacture huge quantities of human insulin in much less time and with much less effort than it took to extract insulin from animals.

Human Genome Project

Scientists from all over the world collaborated on the Human Genome Project, which represents one of the most ambitious projects ever undertaken in science. A **genome** is the complete set of an organism's DNA. The goal of the Human Genome Project was to identify the entire sequence of the nearly three billion bases that make up all the genes in humans. Another goal was to identify the location of every gene on each chromosome.

This project began in 1990. The first goal was completed in 2003 when scientists reported the following discoveries.

- The human genome contains slightly more than three billion bases.
- The average gene consists of 3000 bases.
- The largest known human gene consists of 2.4 million bases.

- The total number of genes is estimated at 30,000.
- About 99.9 percent of the bases are exactly the same in all people.
- The functions are unknown for more than 50 percent of discovered genes.
- The genes are predominantly composed of the DNA building blocks G and C.
- Genes appear to be concentrated in random areas along the genome.
- Chromosome #1 has the most genes (2968), and the Y chromosome in males has the fewest (231).

Ethical Concerns

Although genetic engineering has proven to be extremely beneficial to humans, concerns have been raised about its potential misuse. Many people worry about how personal genetic information could be used. For example, an insurance company may refuse coverage to a person identified as having a gene for a particular disease. Another concern is that genes spliced into bacteria may create organisms that could cause epidemics. Aware of these concerns, scientists take precautions to make sure that genetic engineering experiments are carried out under strict guidelines and carefully supervised conditions.

Lesson 5

Review

Darken the circle for the best answer.

1. Which represents a pair of bases that can be found in DNA?

Ⓐ G-C

Ⓑ G-A

Ⓒ G-T

Ⓓ T-C

2. Which represents the correct flow of genetic information in a cell?

Ⓐ protein → trait → DNA → RNA

Ⓑ trait → DNA → protein → RNA

Ⓒ RNA → trait → DNA → protein

Ⓓ DNA → RNA → protein → trait

3. How many genes did the Human Genome Project determine are present in all of a person's chromosomes?

Ⓐ 1 million

Ⓑ 100,000

Ⓒ 30,000

Ⓓ 3,000

4. A mutation is defined as a change in

Ⓐ a protein.

Ⓑ DNA.

Ⓒ RNA.

Ⓓ a disease.

5. Which phrase describes a genome?

Ⓐ a disease caused by a mutation

Ⓑ a gene inserted into a bacterial chromosome

Ⓒ the complete set of genes in an organism

Ⓓ the genes that are responsible for an individual's traits

6. How is recombinant DNA made?

Ⓐ Pieces of DNA from two different species are combined.

Ⓑ Mutations are produced in the DNA.

Ⓒ The chromosomes are broken into smaller pieces.

Ⓓ All the DNA is changed into RNA.

7. How is genetic engineering different from natural reproduction?

_____

_____

_____

8. A human cell contains 46 chromosomes that contain 3.2 billion bases. On average, how many bases are in each chromosome?

_____

9. How is it possible for a mutation not to produce any visible effect in an organism?

_____

_____

_____

Lesson 5   DNA Replication

Cells divide to produce new cells. Before a cell divides, each chromosome must be duplicated. A copy is made of each chromosome. When a cell divides, a complete set of chromosomes passes into each of the two cells. As a result, each new cell receives a complete set of hereditary information. The duplication of a chromosome means that the DNA must be copied. The process of copying DNA is called replication. During replication, the two chains of the double helix separate. A new chain is then made on each of the original chains. The following diagram illustrates the process of replication.

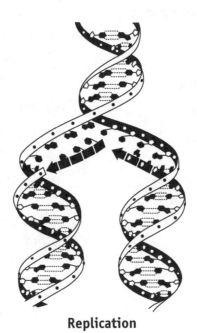

Replication

During replication, if A is present on one chain, then only T can be paired with it. Likewise, if C is present on a chain, then only G can be paired with it. Assume that you have the following sequence of bases in one chain of DNA.

G—T—T—C—A—A—C—G—C—T—A—A—G—G—T—A—C—C

What will be the sequence of bases in the chain that is made during replication from the above DNA chain?

_____

Lesson 5   RNA Transcription

DNA makes RNA in a process called transcription. During transcription, the two strands of the DNA double helix separate just as they do in replication.

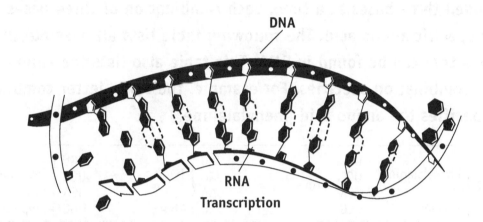

The bases form pairs. For example, if the base C is present in DNA, then only the base G can pair with it in the RNA. Likewise, if the base T is present in DNA, then only the base A can pair with it in the RNA. There is, however, one difference in the base pairs that form during transcription. RNA contains the base uracil (U) in place of the base T. RNA does not contain any T. Therefore, if the base A is present in DNA, then only the base U can pair with it in the RNA.

Assume that you have the following sequence of bases in one chain of DNA.

G—T—T—C—A—A—C—G—C—T—A—A—G—G—T—A—C—C

What will be the sequence of bases in the RNA chain that is made during transcription from the above DNA chain?

Lesson 5   Protein Synthesis

RNA directs the production of proteins in a process called translation. Proteins are made by joining building blocks called amino acids. The genetic information in RNA is decoded three bases at a time. Each combination of three bases in RNA codes for a specific amino acid. The following table lists all possible three-letter combinations that can be found in RNA. This table also lists the amino acid each three-letter combination specifies. For example, the three-letter combination U—U—U specifies the amino acid phenylalanine.

UUU UUC } Phenylalanine UUA UUG } Leucine	UCU UCC UCA UCG } Serine	UAU UAC } Tyrosine UAA UAG } Stop	UGU UGC } Cysteine UGA } Stop UGG } Tryptophan
CUU CUC CUA CUG } Leucine	CCU CCC CCA CCG } Proline	CAU CAC } Histidine CAA CAG } Glutamine	CGU CGC CGA CGG } Arginine
AUU AUC AUA } Isoleucine AUG } Start	ACU ACC ACA ACG } Threonine	AAU AAC } Asparagine AAA AAG } Lysine	AGU AGC } Serine AGA AGG } Arginine
GUU GUC GUA GUG } Valine	GCU GCC GCA GCG } Alanine	GAU GAC } Aspartic acid GAA GAG } Glutamic acid	GGU GGC GGA GGG } Glycine

Use the sequence of bases in RNA that you made in the previous activity to determine the sequence of amino acids that it specifies. Hint: Your sequence should consist of six amino acids, starting with glutamine.

RNA bases from previous activity:

_____

amino acid sequence:

_____

Lesson 5   **Mutations**

You learned that a mutation involves a change in the DNA. The change can be as simple as replacing one base in the DNA with a different base. Assume that you have the following sequence of bases in one chain of DNA.

G—T—T—C—A—A—C—G—C—T—A—A—G—G—T—A—C—C

1. Change any one base in the above sequence of DNA bases. Write out the new sequence that shows the mutation.

_____

2. What will be the sequence of bases in the RNA chain that is made during transcription from your mutated DNA chain above?

_____

3. What will be the sequence of amino acids that your RNA sequence above determines? Use the table from the activity on Protein Synthesis.

_____

4. How does the above sequence of amino acids differ from the sequence you determined in the activity on Protein Synthesis?

_____

_____

5. Why is it possible to change a base in DNA and yet not have it affect the sequence of amino acids that is made? Hint: Notice how many three-letter combinations of RNA bases specify the same amino acid.

_____

_____

_____

Lesson 5, Mutations
Science 8, SV 9781419034367

Lesson 5   Experiment: Extracting DNA

Taking out the DNA from cells is a rather simple process, as you can see by doing the following experiment. You will use a liquid detergent to break open cells to release the DNA. You will then use meat tenderizer to break down proteins, which are also found in chromosomes. This will leave the DNA that you can then pick up with a wooden skewer.

What You Need

measuring cup
dried split peas
teaspoon
table salt
blender
tablespoon
liquid detergent
narrow glass container
meat tenderizer
wooden skewer
rubbing alcohol
water
strainer

Procedure

1. Place half a cup of split peas, a cup of cold water, and a $\frac{1}{4}$ teaspoon of table salt in a blender.

2. Blend on the high setting for 15 seconds. The pea "soup" should be so thick that you cannot see through it. If your "soup" is too thin, add more peas and blend again.

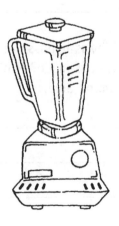

3. Pour the pea "soup" through a strainer and collect the liquid in the measuring cup.

4. Add 2 tablespoons of the liquid detergent. Allow the mixture to stand for 15 minutes.

Experiment: Extracting DNA (cont'd.)

5. Pour some of the mixture into the glass container.

6. Add a pinch of meat tenderizer.

7. Use the skewer to stir the mixture very gently.

8. Tilt the glass container and slowly pour the alcohol down the side so that it forms a layer on top of the greenish mixture. Pour about the same amount of alcohol as you have greenish mixture.

9. Insert the skewer into the alcohol-pea mixture and gently swirl it.

Results and Analysis

Describe what collects on the skewer.

_____

_____

_____

_____

_____

_____

Conclusion

What conclusion can you draw based on your observations?

_____

_____

_____

_____

_____

_____

Lesson 6 Regulation and Behavior

Have you ever been rewarded for exemplary behavior? Perhaps your family took you to watch your favorite team play because you studied hard and did well on all your final exams. There may have been a time, however, when you were reprimanded for unacceptable behavior. For example, you may have been told that you were not allowed to go with friends to the movies because you watched television rather than study for your test. All the activities that you do, including studying and watching television, are known as behavior.

Behavior

Behavior is the manner in which an organism acts. A **behavior** can be defined as an action or series of actions that an animal performs in response to a stimulus. A **stimulus** is anything that causes a response. The stimulus for a particular behavior may be something in the organism's environment. For example, you might jump after you suddenly hear a loud noise.

To respond, an organism must have some way to detect a stimulus. Humans have several senses that can detect a stimulus. These include the sense of sight, hearing, touch, taste, and smell. All these senses continuously pick up stimuli and send the information to the brain. The brain interprets the information and then regulates the responses or behavior.

Sense of Sight

Your eyes are a complex sensory organ. A **sensory organ** is an organ that is specialized to detect a stimulus. Your eyes allow you to detect an object around you. You see an object when it reflects or sends visible light to your eyes. The following illustration shows how light enters your eyes.

Key Terms

behavior—an action or series of actions that an animal performs in response to a stimulus

stimulus—anything that causes a response

sensory organ—an organ that is specialized to detect a stimulus

retina—the inner layer of specialized cells found at the back of the eye

photoreceptor—a specialized cell in the retina that detects light and then sends signals to the brain

cochlea—a fluid-filled structure that makes up part of the inner ear

papilla—a tiny bump on the tongue that may contain a taste bud

olfactory cell—a nerve cell that detects chemical substances in the air

homeostasis—the maintenance of a constant internal environment despite changes in the external environment

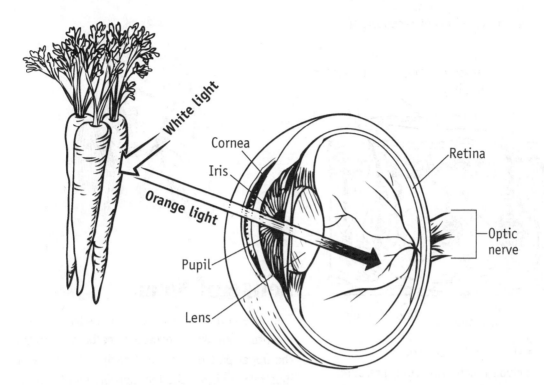

White light

Orange light

Cornea

Iris

Pupil

Lens

Retina

Optic nerve

Notice in the illustration above that the front of the eye is protected by a clear membrane called the *cornea*. Light enters the eye through an opening in the cornea called the *pupil*. The light next passes through a *lens*, which focuses the light on the retina. The **retina** is the inner layer of specialized cells found at the back of the eye. These cells are called **photoreceptors** because they detect light and then send signals to the brain. The brain interprets these signals and forms the images that you see.

There are two kinds of photoreceptors. One kind is known as a rod. Rod cells are sensitive to dim light. These cells send signals to the brain that are interpreted as black-and-white images. Rods are important for night vision. The second kind of photoreceptor is called a cone. Cone cells are sensitive to bright light. These cells send signals to the brain that are interpreted as color images with details. Both rods and cones send their signals to the brain by way of the optic nerve that leaves the back of the eye.

Sense of Hearing

Ears are sensory organs specialized for hearing. Each ear consists of three parts—an outer, middle, and inner portion, as shown in the following illustration.

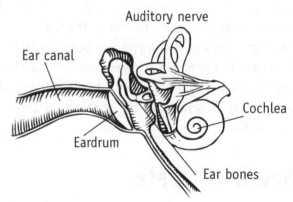

Auditory nerve

Ear canal

Eardrum

Cochlea

Ear bones

The outer ear captures sounds that travel as waves in the air. The waves are funneled through the ear canal to the eardrum. The waves make the eardrum vibrate. The vibrating eardrum then makes tiny bones in the middle ear vibrate. One of these bones vibrates against the cochlea. The **cochlea** is a fluid-filled structure that makes up part of the inner ear. Vibrations of the bone make waves in the fluid inside the cochlea. Nerve cells in the cochlea change these vibrations into signals that are sent to the brain. The brain then interprets these signals as sounds.

Sense of Touch

The skin has several different types of nerve cells, or receptors, to detect stimuli. Each kind of receptor detects a different kind of stimulus. The following illustration shows the various kinds of receptors in the skin.

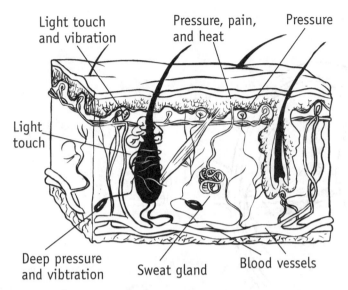

Light touch and vibration

Pressure, pain, and heat

Pressure

Light touch

Deep pressure and vibration

Sweat gland

Blood vessels

Notice that the skin can detect various sensations. These include touch, vibration, pressure, heat, and pain. If a pressure receptor is stimulated, then it sends a signal to the brain. The brain interprets this signal as a pressure being applied to that area. If a deep pressure receptor is stimulated, the brain may send back a signal to move that part of the body away from the object that is causing the pressure.

Sense of Taste

Your tongue is covered with tiny bumps called **papillae**. Most papillae contain taste buds. A taste bud is a specialized nerve cell that can detect a particular stimulus. These nerve cells can detect four basic tastes: sweetness, sourness, saltiness, and bitterness. When you put something in your mouth, hundreds of taste buds are stimulated. Some of these may be taste buds for saltiness, while others are taste buds for sweetness. All these taste buds send signals to the brain. The brain combines the information from all the taste buds to produce a single taste that you may or may not like.

Sense of Smell

The nose contains receptors for smells. These receptors, known as **olfactory cells**, are located in the upper part of the nasal cavity. The following illustration shows the location of the olfactory cells.

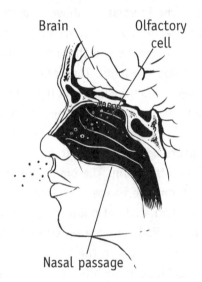

Brain

Olfactory cell

Nasal passage

Olfactory cells line the nasal cavity. These cells are sensory receptors that react to chemicals in the air. Chemical substances in the air are inhaled through the nostrils. These substances travel up the nose where they stimulate olfactory cells. The olfactory cells then send signals to the brain. The brain interprets these signals as odors.

The sense of taste and smell work closely together. The brain combines information from both taste buds and olfactory cells. This combined information gives you sensations of flavor. These sensations are not produced to the same extent when you have a cold. The nasal passages may be partially blocked, preventing chemicals in the air from reaching the olfactory cells. Therefore, the brain does not receive as much information from the olfactory cells when you have a cold. Without this information, the brain does not produce the same sensation as it normally does.

Feedback

You learned that the senses continuously provide information to the brain. The brain interprets all this information and regulates the appropriate response. The brain and the senses operate under a feedback system. A feedback system is a cycle of events in which information from one process affects another process.

For example, consider what happens when you shake some salt on your food and then place it in your mouth. Taste buds for saltiness are stimulated and send information to the brain. The brain interprets this information as not enough salt was added. Your brain sends signals for you to add more salt. The taste buds again send information to the brain. This time, the brain interprets the information as just the right amount of salt was added. You can now enjoy your food because of the feedback that occurred between your taste buds and brain.

The brain regulates responses or behavior in a process called homeostasis. **Homeostasis** is the maintenance of a constant internal environment despite changes in the external environment. For example, receptors in the skin can detect heat. If too many receptors are stimulated, the brain may interpret this information as the external temperature being too high. The brain will then send signals so that actions are taken to keep the body's temperature from rising. The brain will send signals to sweat glands to increase their activity. The brain will also send signals to blood vessels near the surface of the body, instructing them to dilate or open wider. This increases blood flow to parts of the body near the surface. By increasing blood flow, more heat is lost through the skin.

Lesson 6

Review

~~~~~~

Darken the circle for the best answer.

1. Three stimuli that the skin detects include
   (A) heat, pressure, and smell.
   (B) temperature, pressure, and pain.
   (C) pressure, sound, and heat.
   (D) touch, light, and smell.

2. Which structure sends signals to the brain so that sounds are heard?
   (A) papilla
   (B) olfactory cell
   (C) cornea
   (D) cochlea

3. Identify the structure that contains photoreceptors.
   (A) retina
   (B) lens
   (C) optic nerve
   (D) skin

4. Which is an example of how homeostasis operates?
   (A) A furnace continuously operates during the winter.
   (B) An air conditioner turns on during a hot summer day.
   (C) A sprinkler system turns on when it is raining.
   (D) A car's engine shuts off at a stoplight.

5. Which of the following structures in the eye allow you to see the world in color?
   (A) lenses
   (B) corneas
   (C) rods
   (D) cones

6. Which sense functions closely with taste to detect the flavor of food?
   (A) touch
   (B) sight
   (C) smell
   (D) hearing

7. Explain why you have trouble seeing colors as clearly at night as you do during the day.

   _____

   _____

8. Why is feedback important for the brain to regulate responses and behavior?

   _____

   _____

   _____

Lesson 6   Focusing the Light

The first illustration shows how the lens correctly bends the light so that it falls on the retina. As a result, the light is focused on the correct spot. The second and third illustrations show what happens in a person who is nearsighted and in a person who is farsighted. Use these illustrations to answer the questions that follow.

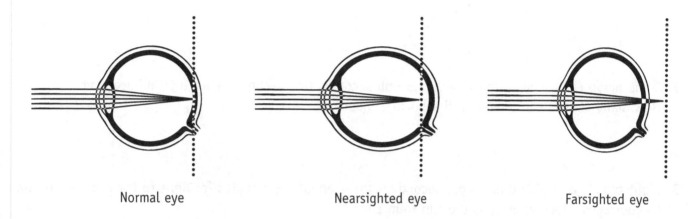

Normal eye   Nearsighted eye   Farsighted eye

1. Describe what the problem is in a person who is nearsighted. Explain what eyeglasses must do to correct this problem.

_____

_____

2. Describe what the problem is in a person who is farsighted. Explain what eyeglasses must do to correct this problem.

_____

_____

3. The lens is an oval-shaped piece of clear material that allows light to pass through it. The lens must continuously change its shape in order to focus light on the retina. Notice in the above illustrations that a tissue is connected to both the upper and lower parts of the lens. What type of tissue do you think this is? Explain your answer.

_____

_____

_____

Lesson 6   Mathematics and the Senses

The following problems involve calculations that deal with the senses. Solve each problem.

1. Sound travels about 760 miles per hour. How far does sound travel in 1 second?

2. Some nerve cells send a signal every 2.5 milliseconds. One second equals 1000 milliseconds. How many signals can a nerve cell send in 2.5 seconds?

3. Light travels at 186,000 miles per second. It takes about 8.5 minutes for light to travel from the sun to your eyes. How far away is the sun from Earth?

4. A nerve cell can be quite long. For example, a nerve can reach a length of 3 feet, stretching from your toe to your spinal cord. If a nerve signal travels at 15 feet/second, how long will it take the signal to go from your toe to your spinal cord?

5. A human sheds about 1.5 pounds of dead skin cells every year. How many pounds of skin has a 60-year-old person shed over his or her lifetime?

Lesson 6   It Doesn't Smell Anymore!

Read the following passage and then answer the questions.

The senses of taste and smell are closely linked to one another. The loss of one will often result in the loss of the other. For many people the problem may be a minor annoyance because they are saddened by the loss of the scent of a rose or a favorite cooking aroma. But for others, the loss of taste and smell can actually be quite a serious matter. The inability to smell a gas leak, a smoldering fire, or other noxious odors like spoiled food can be very dangerous.

Taste and smell disorders are common. It is estimated that more than two million Americans have a smell and taste disorder. The most common causes for loss of sense of taste and smell are the result of a nasal obstruction, such as the common cold, breathing allergies, and nasal congestion from irritants like cigarette smoke and pollutants. A blow to the head can upset your sense of smell because the nerves of smell may be damaged or blocked by scar tissue. Occupational exposure to chemicals may also lessen the sense of smell. Certain medications can also affect the sense of smell. As we get older, the sense of smell becomes less accurate.

A nasal examination with a nasal telescope, which is called an endoscope, illuminates and magnifies the areas of the nose where problems can occur. An examination with an endoscope will usually indicate the problem and direct a doctor to select an appropriate treatment.

1. How can the loss of smell be dangerous for a person?

_____

_____

_____

_____

2. What are the main reasons people lose their sense of smell?

_____

_____

_____

_____

3. A professional boxer has lost his sense of smell. Why is this not surprising?

_____

_____

_____

_____

4. Criticize the statement "Smell improves with age."

_____

_____

_____

_____

www.harcourtschoolsupply.com
© Harcourt Achieve Inc. All rights reserved.

69

Lesson 6, It Doesn't Smell Anymore!
Science 8, SV 9781419034367

Lesson 6   Experiment: What Do You Taste?

The sense of taste is not as straightforward as it may seem. You learned that taste is closely associated with smell. In addition, a particular food may not taste the same to different people. What tastes good to you may not at all be "tasty" to someone else. Food companies try to influence people to like the taste of a certain product by adding color. Jelly beans are an example. Red color is added to promote a cherry flavor, yellow for lemon, orange for orange, and green for lime. In this experiment, you will investigate whether people can really taste the flavor.

You Will Need

paper towels
pen
4 different colored jelly beans
helper test subject

Procedure

1. Label four paper towels with the numbers 1 through 4.

2. Place one jelly bean of each color on a separate paper towel.

3. Have your test subject eat one of the jelly beans.

4. Ask him or her to write down how the flavor tastes.

5. Repeat steps 3–4 for the remaining jelly beans.

6. Repeat steps 3–4 again, but this time tell your subject to close his or her eyes. Your subject must not know what color jelly bean he or she is eating. You can tell your subject that he or she will taste the same jelly beans as before, but in a different order.

7. After your subject has finished eating each jelly bean, ask him or her to open his or her eyes. Keep the remaining jelly beans out of sight.

8. Ask your subject what color jelly bean he or she just ate. Your subject can refer to the notes about flavors from the earlier tasting.

Experiment: What Do You Taste? (cont'd.)

Results and Analysis

1. Did your subject make any mistakes when he or she could not see the color of the jelly bean?

_____

_____

_____

2. Was one color the most difficult to identify for its flavor?

_____

_____

_____

Conclusion

What conclusion can you draw from your results?

_____

_____

_____

_____

Lesson 7 Populations and Ecosystems

All organisms interact with their environment. To make it easier to study, scientists arrange the environment into different levels. An organism is the simplest level. The next level is a **species**, which includes all the organisms that can mate with one another and produce fertile offspring. All humans, for example, are members of a species called *Homo sapiens*. The next level is a population. A

population consists of all the members of the same species that live in a specific area. For example, all the people who live in your town, village, or city make up its population.

Populations are organized into a community. A **community** includes different populations that live in the same place. The next level of organization is an ecosystem. An **ecosystem** includes all the populations in a specific area as well as the nonliving factors that are found in the community.

Key Terms

species—a group of organisms that have common features and can mate to produce fertile offspring

population—all the members of the same species that live in the same place

community—the different populations that live in the same place

ecosystem—all the organisms within a community and the nonliving things with which they interact

biotic factor—a living component in the environment

abiotic factor—a nonliving component in the environment

evaporation—the change of a substance from a liquid to a gas

transpiration—the loss of water from the leaves of plants

condensation—the change of a substance from a gas to a liquid

precipitation—any form of water that falls to Earth from the clouds

respiration—the process of using oxygen to break down sugars and release energy

combustion—the burning of a substance such as wood or coal

decomposition—the breakdown of substances into simpler substances

photosynthesis—the process by which plants use light energy to change carbon dioxide and water into sugars and oxygen

nitrogen fixation—the process by which bacteria change nitrogen gas into a form plants can use

limiting factor—any natural resource that limits the size of a population

carrying capacity—the largest population that an environment can support at any given time

Biotic and Abiotic Factors

An ecosystem is a level of organization that includes both living and nonliving things. Any living component in an environment is called a **biotic factor**. Biotic factors include animals, plants, bacteria, protists, and fungi. Any nonliving component in the environment is called an **abiotic factor**. Important abiotic factors include temperature, oxygen concentration, humidity, amount of sunlight, and nitrogen availability. The importance of each abiotic factor varies from ecosystem to ecosystem. For example, water is a much more important biotic factor in a desert ecosystem than in a tropical rain forest.

Abiotic factors vary not only from ecosystem to ecosystem but also from time to time within the same ecosystem. For example, temperatures in a desert are quite different from those in a tundra ecosystem found in the Arctic. However, even within a desert, the temperature can drop from 38°C (100°F) during the day to 7°C (45°F) at night.

The Water Cycle

Some abiotic factors are recycled and reused. These factors include water, oxygen, carbon, and nitrogen. The recycling of any one of these factors usually involves several ecosystems. The following illustration shows how ocean, lake, and forest ecosystems all play a role in recycling water.

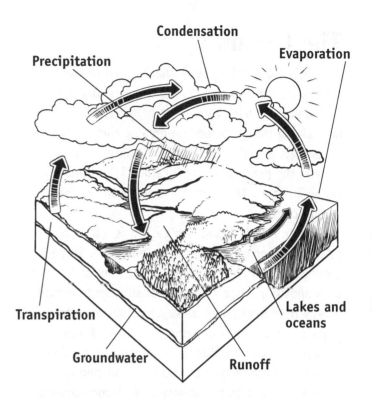

Several processes are involved in recycling water. During **evaporation**, water is changed by the sun's heat from a liquid to a vapor or gas. Water also passes from Earth to the atmosphere by transpiration. **Transpiration** is the loss of water from the leaves of plants.

Water is recycled back to Earth through condensation and precipitation. **Condensation** occurs when water changes from a gas to a liquid as it is cooled. **Precipitation** is any form of water that falls to Earth from the clouds. Precipitation includes rain, snow, sleet, and hail. Some of the precipitation that falls on land flows into streams, ponds, rivers, and oceans as runoff. Some of the water also seeps into the ground and is stored in spaces within and between the rocks. This water contributes to the groundwater, which can be used for drinking. Some of the groundwater also returns back to the soil, streams, rivers, and oceans.

The Carbon Cycle

Carbon is the building block that is used to build substances known as *organic compounds*. Organic compounds include proteins, carbohydrates, and fats. Living things depend on organic compounds for energy, growth, and reproduction. The carbon cycle is the process by which carbon is recycled through nature. The illustration below shows the carbon cycle.

Notice in this figure that carbon is returned to the atmosphere through three processes. These processes include respiration, combustion, and decomposition. Organisms use **respiration** to obtain energy from foods, such as sugars. Carbon dioxide is produced during respiration and released into the atmosphere. **Combustion** is the process of burning a substance, such as coal or wood. Combustion releases carbon dioxide into the atmosphere. **Decomposition** is the breaking down of substances into simpler substances. For example, bacteria decompose the remains of dead organisms. Like respiration and combustion, decomposition releases carbon dioxide into the atmosphere.

Photosynthesis is the only process that removes carbon dioxide from the atmosphere. During **photosynthesis**, plants use the energy from sunlight to change carbon dioxide and water into sugars and oxygen. Most animals get the energy they need by eating plants.

For millions of years, the processes that return carbon to the atmosphere have been in balance with photosynthesis. However, during the past 100 years or so, humans have greatly increased the rate at which combustion occurs. As a result, more carbon is being added to the atmosphere than can be recycled back to Earth by photosynthesis. Scientists are investigating how this change in the carbon cycle might affect populations and ecosystems.

The Nitrogen Cycle

In addition to water, carbon, and oxygen, nitrogen is also important to living things. Organisms need nitrogen to build proteins. The nitrogen cycle is the process by which nitrogen is recycled through nature. The illustration on the following page shows the nitrogen cycle.

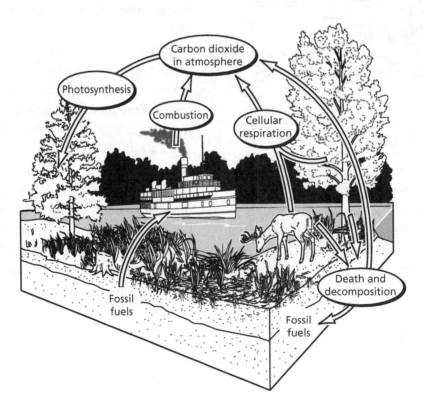

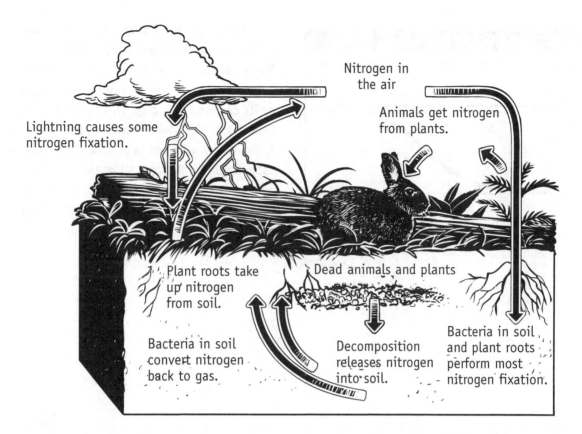

Nitrogen in the air

Lightning causes some nitrogen fixation.

Animals get nitrogen from plants.

Plant roots take up nitrogen from soil.

Dead animals and plants

Bacteria in soil convert nitrogen back to gas.

Decomposition releases nitrogen into soil.

Bacteria in soil and plant roots perform most nitrogen fixation.

Although the air is about 78 percent nitrogen gas, most organisms cannot use this gas directly. Bacteria in the soil and on plant roots must first change the nitrogen gas into a form that plants can use. This process is called **nitrogen fixation**. Decomposition also releases a form of nitrogen that plants can use. Other organisms can then get the nitrogen they need by eating plants or other organisms that eat plants.

Limiting Factors

Most populations produce more offspring than will survive. For example, a single female salmon can lay as many as 10,000 eggs. If all these eggs are fertilized and develop into adult salmon, there will be about 5000 females. If each female lays 10,000 eggs, then the second generation would have 50,000,000 salmon. However, the size of the salmon population remains about the same from year to year.

Populations do not grow without stopping because the environment limits their numbers. The environment contains a limited amount of food, water, living space, and other resources. Any resource

that is scarce and limits the size of a population is called a **limiting factor**. Any single resource, such as water, can be a limiting factor to a population's size.

The following graph shows what would happen to the size of a population if there were no limiting factors. Notice that the number of individuals would continue to increase at a very rapid rate.

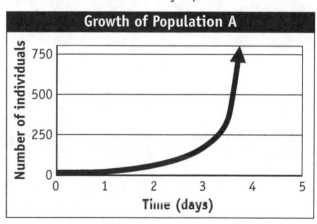

Growth of Population A

Limiting factors keep a population from growing at such a fast rate. Instead, a population reaches a certain size and then stops increasing. The graph on the next page shows how limiting factors determine the number of individuals that make up a population.

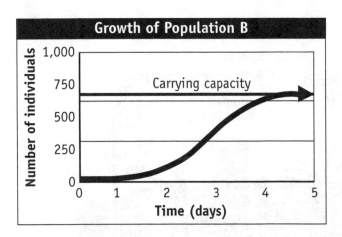

Growth of Population B

Number of individuals

Carrying capacity

Time (days)

This graph shows that a population grows slowly at first, then undergoes a rapid rate of growth, and finally reaches its maximum size. The largest population that an environment can support is known as its **carrying capacity**. In the graph, the carrying capacity of the environment is about 650 individuals. A population may get larger than the carrying capacity, but only for a short time. A limiting factor will cause the population to return to its carrying capacity. As a result, the ecosystem will remain in balance.

Lesson 7   Review

Darken the circle by the best answer.

1. Which can be an abiotic limiting factor?
   - (A) parasites
   - (B) decomposers
   - (C) sunlight
   - (D) plants

2. Which process removes carbon from the atmosphere in the carbon cycle?
   - (A) respiration
   - (B) combustion
   - (C) transpiration
   - (D) photosynthesis

3. Nitrogen fixation is the process by which
   - (A) proteins are made.
   - (B) bacteria convert nitrogen into a form plants can use.
   - (C) nitrogen is returned to the atmosphere.
   - (D) decomposers recycle nitrogen into the soil.

4. As a population approaches the carrying capacity of its environment,
   - (A) more organisms move into the population.
   - (B) organisms get larger.
   - (C) more offspring are produced to increase the population size.
   - (D) resources become limited.

5. Clouds form in the atmosphere through the process of
   - (A) condensation.
   - (B) precipitation.
   - (C) respiration.
   - (D) decomposition.

6. Burning gasoline in a car affects the
   - (A) water cycle.
   - (B) carbon cycle.
   - (C) nitrogen cycle.
   - (D) process of decomposition.

7. Which level of organization includes abiotic factors?
   - (A) species
   - (B) population
   - (C) community
   - (D) ecosystem

8. How do limiting factors affect the carrying capacity of an environment?

   _____

   _____

9. What role do humans have in the carbon cycle?

   _____

   _____

Lesson 7

A Population and Ecosystem Crossword Puzzle

Across

3. what bacteria fix for plants to use

5. process that uses light energy to make sugars

11. maximum size of a population that the environment can support

12. all the members of a species that live in the same area

13. loss of water from leaves

Down

1. all the organisms in a community and the abiotic factors

2. living component in the environment

4. change of a substance from a liquid to a gas

6. process that uses oxygen to obtain energy

7. an abiotic factor

8. burning

9. substance that is recycled in nature

10. involves precipitation and runoff

Lesson 7   Population Growth

The graph below shows the growth of a population of a single-celled organism called paramecium. These organisms were grown in a test tube to which food was occasionally added. Use this graph to answer the questions that follow.

1. When did this population reach the carrying capacity of its environment?

   _____

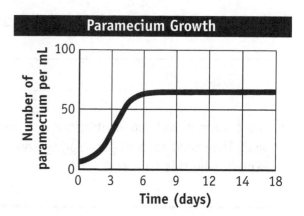

2. What is the carrying capacity of the test tube as long as food is added?

   _____

   _____

3. What is the limiting factor that keeps the paramecium population at this carrying capacity?

   _____

4. Predict what will happen to this population if no more food is added.

   _____

5. Predict what would likely happen to this population if it is placed in a larger test tube and more food is added.

   _____

   _____

6. Predict what the size of this population will be on day 25 if the same conditions are maintained.

   _____

Lesson 7   The Carbon Cycle

The graph below shows the concentration of carbon dioxide in the atmosphere between 1958 and 1990. Use this graph to answer the questions that follow,

1. What conclusion can you draw from this graph?

   _____

   _____

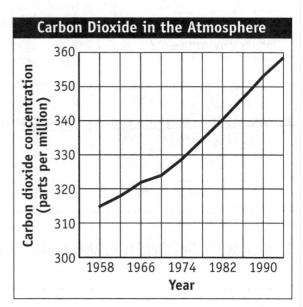

Carbon Dioxide in the Atmosphere

2. The carbon dioxide concentrations rise and fall each year. They tend to drop each spring and summer. Explain why this happens.

   _____

   _____

3. In contrast, the carbon dioxide concentrations tend to rise each fall and winter. Explain why this happens.

   _____

   _____

4. Carbon dioxide is called a greenhouse gas because it contributes to global warming. Global warming is the gradual increase in Earth's average temperature. Based on the graph shown on this page, draw another graph to predict how Earth's average temperature changed over this 32-year period.

Lesson 7

Experiment: Estimating the Size of a Population

Scientists who study ecosystems often need to know the size of a population. However, counting all the organisms that make up a population is impossible. Animals can be difficult to count because they always move around and hide. Therefore, scientists must rely upon other ways to determine the size of a population. In this experiment, you will use one such method called the mark-recapture method.

You Will Need

helper
pencil
ruler
paper
dried beans
paper bags
permanent marker

Procedure

1. Prepare a data table like the one below.

Number of animals in first capture	Total number of animals in recapture	Number of marked animals in recapture	Calculated estimate of population	Actual total population

2. Have your helper place an unknown number of beans in the paper bag.

3. Reach into the bag and remove a handful of beans.

4. Count the number of beans you removed from the bag. Record this number in the data table under "Number of animals in first capture."

5. Use the marker to place an X on each bean you removed from the bag. Allow the marks to dry completely.

6. Place the marked beans back into the bag.

Experiment: Estimating the Size of a Population (cont'd.)

7. Gently mix the beans in the bag. Again reach into the bag and remove a handful of beans.

8. Count the number of beans you removed from the bag. Record this number in the data table under "Total number of animals in recapture."

9. Count the number of beans in your "recapture" that are marked. Record this number in the data table under "Number of marked animals in recapture."

10. Calculate the estimated size of the population by using the following equation.

$$\frac{\text{number of beans in recapture} \times \text{number of beans marked}}{\text{number of marked beans in recapture}} = \text{estimate of population}$$

11. Place all the beans in the bag. Empty the bag and count all the beans. Record this number in the data table under "Actual total population."

Results and Analysis

1. How close was your estimate to the actual number of beans?

_____

_____

2. If your estimate was not close to the actual number, what might you do to get a better estimate?

_____

_____

Conclusion

What conclusion can you draw based on your observations?

_____

_____

Lesson 8 Diversity and Adaptations of Organisms

In 1831, a young Englishman named Charles Darwin began a five-year voyage around the world. The ship he sailed on was called the *Beagle*. Darwin had signed on as the ship's naturalist, which is a scientist who studies nature. During this long voyage, Darwin collected thousands of plant and animal specimens. He was amazed at some of the unusual organisms he observed. Based on his observations, Darwin concluded that species change over time. He also developed a theory to explain how these changes occur. In this lesson, you will learn what Darwin discovered about the living things that inhabit this world.

Darwin's Trip

Not all scientific discoveries are the result of careful planning. Darwin's discoveries are an example. In fact, his trip was not even planned. Darwin's career as a naturalist developed simply because he did not know what he wanted to do in life. His father wanted him to become a doctor. This was only natural as Darwin's father was a doctor. However, Darwin could not stand the sight of blood. He later wrote that he had to run out of a class in medical school while he was observing an operation.

Realizing that Darwin could never become a doctor, his father decided to send him to college to become a minister. Darwin graduated, but he had no interest in becoming a minister. Rather, he was more interested in plants and animals. In fact, he spent a lot of his time in college taking trips with a professor named John Henslow to observe nature. These trips sparked Darwin's desire to become a naturalist.

The position of naturalist aboard the *Beagle* was first offered to Henslow. However, he had to decline because his wife was not well. Henslow recommended Darwin in his place. Although his father strongly objected at first, Darwin was finally able to get his permission to go. The voyage began from England on December 27, 1831, and returned to England on October 2, 1836.

Key Terms

biodiversity—the variety and complexity of life that exists on Earth

adaptation—a feature that increases an organism's chances to survive and reproduce

evolution—the gradual change in a species over time

fossil—the remains or physical evidence of an organism that has been preserved by natural processes

natural selection—the process by which evolution is thought to occur

artificial selection—the human practice of breeding plants or animals that have certain desirable traits; also known as selective breeding

speciation—the formation of a new species as a result of evolution

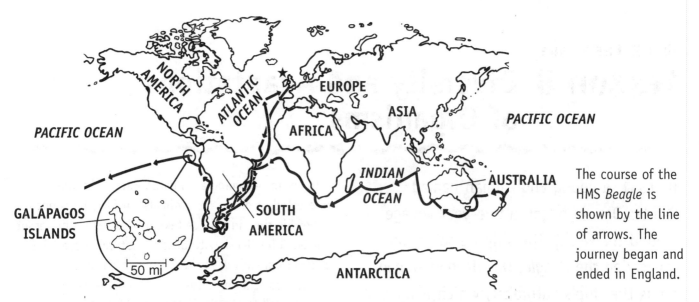

The course of the HMS *Beagle* is shown by the line of arrows. The journey began and ended in England.

Variations and Adaptations

During this long voyage, Darwin collected thousands of plant and animal specimens. He was amazed at some of the unusual organisms he observed. For example, Darwin was impressed by the giant tortoises on the Galápagos Islands, which lie about 600 miles west of Ecuador in South America. These animals can live for almost 100 years, weigh as much as 400 pounds, and grow to nearly 6 feet in length. But what really amazed Darwin was the tremendous diversity of life that exists on Earth.

Across Earth, there are millions of different species. All these organisms point to the biodiversity that exists on Earth. **Biodiversity** is the variety and complexity of life that inhabits Earth. This biodiversity ranges from single cell organisms to complex living things made of trillions of cells, such as humans.

Darwin was not the first scientist to appreciate this biodiversity. However, he was the first scientist to appreciate the diversity that existed even within a single species. At that time, scientists thought that species were unchanging. They also thought that each species had an ideal type. Differences from this ideal type were not important. Darwin, however, recognized the value of these differences or variations in a species.

In some cases, these variations were not very noticeable. Fortunately, Darwin had developed a keen sense of observation as a result of his nature trips with Henslow in England. Darwin noticed small variations among the finches on the Galápagos Islands. The beaks of finches on each island differed from the beaks of finches on the other islands. The finches on one island have a wide, powerful beak, while the finches on another island have a small, narrow beak.

Darwin recognized that each variation was an adaptation. An **adaptation** is a feature that improves an organism's chances to survive and reproduce. The wide, powerful beaks enabled the finches to crack open big, hard seeds, which was their main food source. The small, narrow beaks enabled the other finches to feed on small insects hidden in rocks and twigs.

Two Events

After Darwin returned home from his voyage, he spent more than 20 years struggling with his ideas. He recognized that a huge controversy would erupt if he claimed that species had changed over time. Such a statement would mean that species had evolved. **Evolution** is the gradual change in a species over time. Two events occurred that caused Darwin to change his mind and move more quickly with his work.

First, Darwin read a book about the human population. The book noted that the human population could increase more quickly than the food supply. The graph on the following page shows how the human population and food supply change over time.

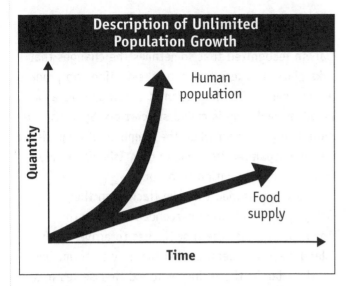

Description of Unlimited Population Growth

Human population

Food supply

Quantity

Time

After reading this book, Darwin realized that the same idea applied to all species, and not just humans. He concluded that only a limited number of individuals survive. The others are victims to starvation, predation, competition, or disease. Darwin reasoned that those who survive have certain adaptations. Those who do not survive lack these adaptations.

Second, Darwin received a letter from a fellow naturalist named Alfred Russel Wallace. In his letter, Wallace had developed the same ideas that Darwin had been thinking about for over 20 years. Friends convinced Darwin that he could no longer wait to tell the public what he had discovered about evolution. In 1859, Darwin's book about evolution was published. It was called *On the Origin of Species by Means of Natural Selection*.

Natural Selection

Scientists have uncovered several lines of evidence that indicate evolution has occurred. For most people, the fossil record is the most convincing. A **fossil** is the remains or physical evidence of an organism that has been preserved by natural processes. Fossils show that species have changed.

The way evolution occurs is a theory. Darwin proposed that evolution occurs through a process he called **natural selection**. This process has four parts.

1. **Overproduction** More individuals are produced in a species than can survive. For example, a single pair of elephants produces about 6

offspring in their lifetimes. In 1000 years, there would be about 86,000,000 elephants descended from just this one pair. Obviously, only a few elephants in each generation survive.

2. **Variations** Every individual has its own combination of traits or characteristics. Each offspring resembles but is not identical to its parents and siblings. Darwin knew that organisms inherited traits from their parents. He also knew that offspring differed from their parents and siblings. However, Darwin did not know how traits were inherited or how variations arose.

3. **Struggle to Survive** Not all individuals have the same chances of survival. For example, some individuals may be more susceptible to disease. Others may be more likely to be captured by a predator. All organisms will struggle to survive. This struggle is sometimes called the "survival of the fittest." Keep in mind that the "fittest" does not mean the biggest or strongest. The "fittest" refers to those individuals who have the adaptations needed to survive.

4. **Successful Reproduction** Those individuals that have the necessary adaptations survive and reproduce. Their offspring are likely to possess the same traits as their parents.

Artificial Selection

Darwin recognized that people had long practiced a selection process. Plants and animals with certain desirable traits were selected for breeding. This process is known as **artificial selection** or selective breeding. Most pets, such as dogs and cats, are the products of artificial selection. This process depends on humans selecting which organisms breed or mate. But does nature do the same, as Darwin suggested in his theory of natural selection?

Natural Selection at Work

Since Darwin's time, scientists have discovered numerous examples of species that have changed as a result of natural selection. Some changes brought about by natural selection have raised serious concerns. An example is the increasing resistance of bacteria to antibiotics. Bacteria are single-celled organisms. Some bacteria can cause serious diseases, such as pneumonia and tetanus.

An antibiotic is often prescribed for a person with a serious bacterial infection. Before the discovery of antibiotics, a person could die from an infection caused by a simple scratch. Today, a serious infection can be cured with an antibiotic. However, antibiotics may not be as effective as they once were. The reason has to do with natural selection.

An antibiotic will kill most bacteria. However, a few bacteria will survive. These survivors are resistant to the antibiotic. These survivors reproduce, passing their resistance on to their offspring. In time, most of the bacteria are resistant to the antibiotic. Because bacteria reproduce so quickly, the time it takes may not be very long. When the antibiotic is used the next time, only a few bacteria are killed. A different antibiotic may then have to be used. The resistance of insects to insecticides is another example of natural selection at work, as shown in the following illustrations.

Speciation

Darwin recognized that sometimes the changes that take place as a result of natural selection can produce a new species. The formation of a new species as a result of evolution is called **speciation**. Speciation is more likely to occur when the members of a species become separated from each other. Islands are ideal locations for speciation to occur.

Darwin reasoned that the finches on the Galápagos Islands were descended from South American finches. The first finches to arrive on the island may have been carried there by a storm. Once on the islands, these finches found themselves in a different environment from the mainland of South America. Over many generations, the finches changed as those that were adapted survived and reproduced. Eventually, the finches on one island became so different from those on another island that they could no longer mate with one another. Whenever this happens, a new species has been formed.

❶ An insecticide will kill most insects, but a few may survive. These survivors have genes that make them resistant to the insecticide.

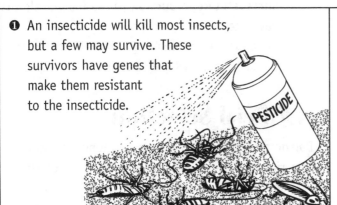

❷ The survivors then reproduce, passing the insecticide-resistant genes to their offspring.

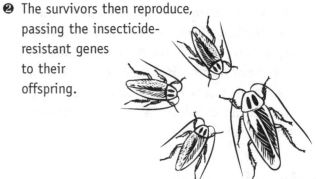

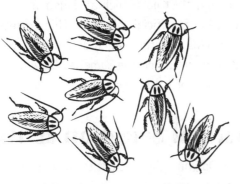

❸ In time, the replacement population of insects is made up mostly of individuals that have the insecticide-resistant genes.

❹ When the same kind of insecticide is used on the insects, only a few are killed because most of them are resistant to that insecticide.

Lesson 8

Review

Darken the circle by the best answer.

1. The process by which humans select organisms with certain desirable traits to mate is known as

   (A) speciation.

   (B) artificial selection.

   (C) natural selection.

   (D) biodiversity.

2. Darwin's theory of how evolution occurs is commonly known as

   (A) overproduction.

   (B) selective breeding.

   (C) survival of the fittest.

   (D) resistance.

3. Which statement about Darwin is correct?

   (A) Darwin was trained as a scientist.

   (B) Darwin developed his theory about evolution during his voyage aboard the *Beagle*.

   (C) Darwin's lifelong ambition was to become a doctor.

   (D) Darwin developed the ability to make close and detailed observations about nature.

4. A gradual change in a species over a long period of time is known as

   (A) evolution.

   (B) adaptation.

   (C) variation.

   (D) biodiversity.

5. The increase in the number of bacteria that are resistant to an antibiotic is the result of

   (A) speciation.

   (B) natural selection.

   (C) artificial selection.

   (D) separation of the bacterial species into different populations.

6. What feature in finches did Darwin closely observe?

   (A) eye color

   (B) wingspan

   (C) beak size and shape

   (D) mating behavior

7. Explain why certain organisms are more likely to survive to adulthood.

   _____

   _____

8. What are the four parts of Darwin's theory of natural selection?

   _____

   _____

   _____

9. What observation was Darwin not able to explain?

   _____

   _____

Lesson 8, Review
Science 8, SV 9781419034367

Lesson 8

The Galápagos Finches

The graph below shows the average beak sizes of a group of finches on one island over several years. Use this graph to answer the questions that follow.

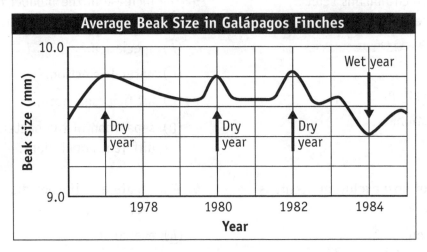

1. What happened to beak size during dry years? Explain why this might have been an adaptation.

_____

_____

_____

2. What happened to beak size during a wet year? Explain why this might have been an adaptation.

_____

_____

_____

3. If beak size is linked to the amount of rainfall, what can you infer about the year 1981 on this island?

_____

_____

Lesson 8

Weight as an Adaptation

The graphs below show information about infant weights at birth and infant deaths by birth weight. Use these graphs to answer the questions that follow.

1. What is the most common birth weight?

_____

_____

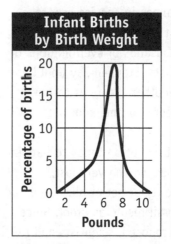

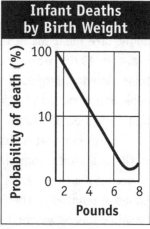

2. At which birth weight is an infant most likely to survive?

_____

_____

3. How do the principles of natural selection help explain why there are more deaths among babies whose birth weights are low than among babies whose birth weights are average?

_____

_____

_____

4. Does a greater birth weight always result in an adaptation? Explain your answer.

_____

_____

Lesson 8

Another Theory of Evolution

Read the following passage and then answer the questions that follow the passage.

According to the theory of natural selection, evolution is a very slow process. Changes in species may take thousands of years, while the origin of a new species might take hundreds of thousands or even millions of years. In 1970, two scientists, Stephen Jay Gould and Niles Eldredge, proposed another theory as to how evolution occurs. Their theory became known as punctuated equilibrium.

This theory states that evolution tends to happen in fits and starts, sometimes moving very fast, sometimes moving very slowly or not at all. Gould and Eldredge pointed to the fossil record as proof. Since Darwin's theory was first proposed, scientists had discovered many fossils. In some cases, the fossil record revealed the evolutionary history of a species.

However, scientists noticed "gaps" in the fossil record. A number of fossils showed little or no change in a species for a long period of time. Then, another fossil showed that the species changed suddenly. Scientists assumed that the fossil record was incomplete. Fossils yet to be discovered would fill these "gaps" and show that the species actually changed gradually and did not undergo a sudden change.

Gould and Eldredge proposed that the fossil record had no "gaps" that would be filled with the discovery of new fossils. They said the fossil record actually showed what happened. According to punctuated equilibrium, a species remains basically the same for long periods of time. Then, a sudden change occurs in response to a dramatic change in the environment. This is then followed by another long period of little or no change. This theory of how evolution occurs is quite different from Darwin's "gradualism."

1. Why is Darwin's theory of natural selection referred to as "gradualism"?

_____

_____

_____

_____

2. How does the theory of punctuated equilibrium differ from natural selection?

_____

_____

_____

_____

3. Is it possible for evolution to occur by both natural selection and punctuated equilibrium? Explain your answer.

_____

_____

_____

_____

_____

Lesson 8   Experiment: Natural Selection

Natural selection operates on the principle that the fittest have a better chance to survive and reproduce. But who are the fittest members of a species? In some cases, the fittest members may be individuals who can run the fastest to capture their prey. In other cases, the fittest may be individuals who can bury themselves in the ground to hibernate during cold weather. In still other cases, the fittest may be individuals who blend in with their backgrounds. Blending in with their background makes them less of a target for their predators. In the following experiment, you will act as a predator. You will go after two types of prey and discover if one has a better chance to avoid you.

You Will Need

helper
hole punch
newspaper
sheet of white paper
paper cup
tweezers
clock or watch with a second hand

Procedure

1. Use a hole punch to make 100 circles from the newspaper and 100 circles from the white paper. Make sure that the circles from the newspaper have printed matter on them.

2. Place all the circles in the paper cup and thoroughly mix them. The printed and plain circles represent two types of prey.

3. Have your helper dump the circles on a sheet of newspaper and spread them out while you are looking in the opposite direction.

4. When your helper gives the signal, turn around and use the tweezers to start picking up as many circles as you can in 15 seconds. After you pick up a circle, place it in the paper cup.

5. Count the number of printed circles and plain circles you placed in the cup.

6. Repeat steps 2–5 two more times.

7. Repeat steps 2–5 three more times. However, dump the circles on a sheet of white paper instead of newspaper.

Experiment: Natural Selection (cont'd.)

Results and Analysis

Use your results to complete the table below. The number of circles represents the number of each type of circle that you placed in the cup. The average is calculated by adding the numbers in each column and then dividing by 3. The percent died is calculated by dividing the average by 100. The percent survived is calculated by subtracting the percent died from 100.

Trial number	Printed Background		Plain Background	
	Number of printed circles	Number of plain circles	Number of printed circles	Number of plain circles
1				
2				
3				
Average				
Percent died				
Percent survived				

Conclusion

What conclusion can you draw based on your results?

_____

_____

_____

Lesson 9 Earth's History and Structure

In the early 1900s, scientists thought that the continents were permanently fixed in their positions. However, a German scientist named Alfred Wegener proposed a theory that the continents once formed a single landmass that broke apart and slowly drifted to their present positions. Wegener based his theory on several pieces of evidence. First, fossils of plants and animals that could not have crossed an ocean were found in both South America and Africa. Fossils are the remains of ancient organisms. Second, South America and Africa look as if they could fit together like pieces of a giant puzzle. Lastly, rock formations in Africa line up with matching ones in South America. Despite this evidence, Wegener's theory was widely rejected by the scientific community.

Continental Drift

Wegener's theory became known as **continental drift**. It wasn't until about thirty years later that technology made it possible to discover evidence to support Wegener's theory. Once scientists were able to

Key Terms

continental drift—the theory that the continents once formed a single landmass

crust—the solid outermost layer of Earth

mantle—the layer between Earth's crust and core

core—the central part of Earth below the mantle

lithosphere—the outermost rigid layer of Earth made of the crust and the solid upper part of the mantle

tectonic plate—a large block of lithosphere

asthenosphere—the molten layer of the mantle on which tectonic plates move

magma—hot, liquid rock

plate tectonics—the theory that Earth's lithosphere is divided into tectonic plates that can move around on top of the asthenosphere

convergent boundary—the location where two tectonic plates push into one another

divergent boundary—the location where two tectonic plates move away from one another

sea-floor spreading—the process by which new oceanic lithosphere forms as magma rises from the mantle and solidifies

transform boundary—the location where two tectonic plates slide past each other

earthquake—the shaking of Earth's surface

seismic wave—a wave of energy that travels through Earth and away from an earthquake in all directions

fault—a break or crack in Earth's surface along which movement has occurred

volcano—an opening in Earth where magma is released

use technology to study Earth more closely, they discovered evidence that our planet is constantly changing.

Earth consists of three layers. The outermost layer is the **crust**. There are two types of crust: continental and oceanic. The **mantle** lies beneath the crust. The **core** is the center of Earth. Both the mantle and core are divided into solid and liquid parts. The crust and the solid upper part of the mantle make up the **lithosphere**. The lithosphere is the uppermost part of Earth and includes all of the crust and the solid upper part of the mantle. The lithosphere is divided into giant moving chunks called **tectonic plates**. You can think of the lithosphere as a giant jigsaw puzzle. Each piece of the puzzle is a tectonic plate, as you can see in the following illustration.

Tectonic plates move because of changes in density within the mantle. Intense heat from Earth's core causes rocks in the mantle to expand. As these rocks expand, they become less dense and rise to the surface. As the rocks get closer to Earth's surface, they cool, become denser, and tend to sink. This rising and sinking of rocks is the cause of plate movement.

Tectonic plates move or float on a denser, molten layer of Earth known as the **asthenosphere**. The asthenosphere is a soft layer of the mantle made up of magma that flows slowly. **Magma** is hot, liquid rock found deep inside Earth but that can sometimes rise to the surface.

Plate Tectonics

The theory that Earth's lithosphere is divided into tectonic plates that can move around on top of the asthenosphere is known as **plate tectonics**. This theory has its origins in Wegener's work in the early 1900s.

The movement of tectonic plates relative to each other can happen in various ways. The location where plates meet is called a boundary. Each type of movement is described in terms of the boundary that forms between the two plates. There are three types of boundaries—convergent, divergent, and transform.

A **convergent boundary** occurs when two tectonic plates push into one another. When two plates converge, they often destroy crust. What happens at a convergent boundary depends on the kind of crust that is at the leading edge of each tectonic plate. Three types of convergent boundaries are possible:

Major Tectonic Plates
1. Pacific plate
2. North American plate
3. Cocos plate
4. Nazca plate
5. South American plate
6. African plate
7. Eurasian plate
8. Indian plate
9. Australian plate
10. Antarctic plate

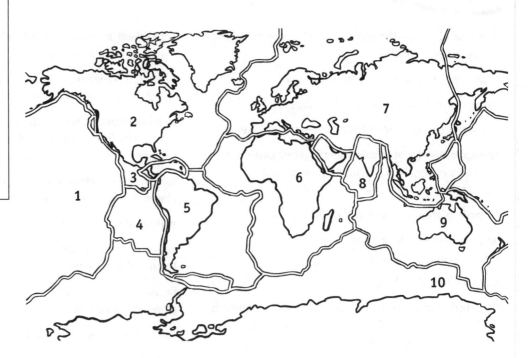

www.harcourtschoolsupply.com
94
Lesson 9, Earth's History and Structure
Science 8, SV 9781419034367

(1) continental-continental boundary, (2) continental-oceanic boundary, and (3) oceanic-oceanic boundary.

A **divergent boundary** occurs when two tectonic plates move away from one another. As a result, a crack or rift forms between them. New crust is formed at a divergent boundary as magma rises up through the gap between the plates. Divergent boundaries have been observed on the ocean floor.

Submerged mountains rise from the ocean floors, including the center of the Atlantic Ocean. These mountains are called mid-ocean ridges, which consist of underwater mountain chains. These ridges are formed by sea-floor spreading. **Sea-floor spreading** is the process by which new oceanic lithosphere forms as magma rises from the mantle and solidifies. Sea-floor spreading occurs when tectonic plates spread apart at a divergent boundary to form a gap which is filled by magma. This process continues, allowing the magma to build up. Eventually, an underwater mountain chain is formed. The following diagram illustrates how sea-floor spreading occurs.

A **transform boundary** occurs when two tectonic plates slide past each other. The San Andreas Fault is a good example of a transform boundary. This fault marks the place where the Pacific and North American plates are sliding past one another.

Earthquakes

An **earthquake** is the shaking of Earth's surface. It occurs when energy stored as pressure in the rocks releases quickly. The pressure can build up as plates press against one another at a convergent boundary, slide by one another at a transform boundary, or stretch and pull away from one another at a divergent boundary. The illustration at the top of page 96 shows how an earthquake can result from the movement of tectonic plates at a transform boundary. When the rocks cannot tolerate the pressure, they break and slip, and give off energy in the form of seismic waves. A **seismic wave** is a wave of energy that travels through Earth and away from an earthquake in all directions.

The break or crack in Earth's surface along which movement has occurred is known as a **fault**. Earthquakes are also associated with folding, which occurs when rock layers crumple into folds during plate collisions. Earthquakes can happen near Earth's surface or far below it. Most earthquakes happen in areas along tectonic plate boundaries where a large number of faults are located. The movement of tectonic plates can also form mountains and volcanoes.

Sea-floor spreading creates new oceanic lithosphere at mid-ocean ridges.

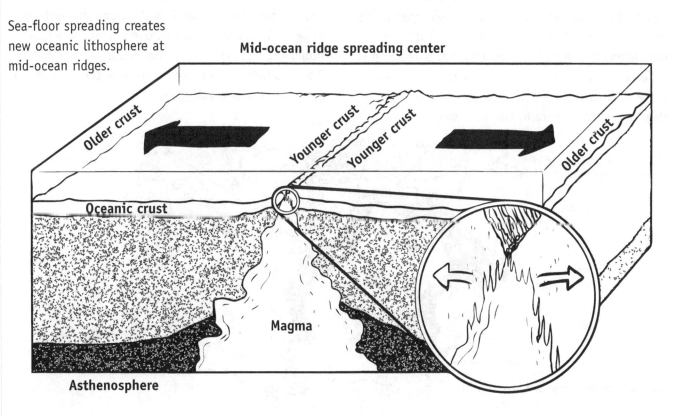

www.harcourtschoolsupply.com
95
Lesson 9, Earth's History and Structure
Science 8, SV 9781419034367

Elastic Rebound and Earthquakes

Before earthquake

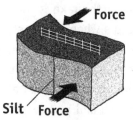

Force

Silt Force

After earthquake

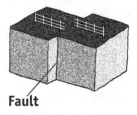

Fault

Mountains and Volcanoes

The highest mountains in the world are known as folded mountains. A folded mountain forms when rock layers are squeezed together and pushed upward. Folded mountains form at convergent boundaries where plates push against one another.

If two continental plates collide, they buckle and thicken. The continental crust is pushed upward, forming folded mountains like the Himalayas. Other examples of folded mountain ranges include the Alps in central Europe and the Ural Mountains in Russia.

If the two plates are oceanic plates, one plate is subducted, or pushed under the other. A deep canyon, or trench, forms under the sea where the plates meet. The bottom edge of the subducted plate melts to form magma as it sinks into the hot mantle. This newly created magma rises toward the surface where it cools and hardens. The result is a chain of volcanoes on the ocean floor. A **volcano** is an opening in Earth where the magma is released. The magma that is released is called lava. As more material accumulates, the tops of the volcanoes become visible. Islands, such as the Hawaiian Islands, were formed this way.

A similar process occurs when a continental plate collides with an oceanic plate. The oceanic plate slides under the continental plate. Chains of volcanic mountains form on the edge of the continental plate.

Hot Spots

For many years, scientists noticed that earthquakes and volcanoes cluster in certain geographic locations known as hot spots. A hot spot stays in the same place even though the plate above it moves. In the case of volcanoes, this results in a chain of volcanoes that are no longer active. The Hawaiian Islands were formed by a hot spot. The island of Hawaii is no longer over the hot spot.

The boundary of the Pacific plate is a hot spot called the Ring of Fire because it contains more than 75 percent of all volcanoes. The ring is an arc that reaches from New Zealand, north along the eastern edge of Asia, across the Aleutian Islands, and down along the western coast of North and South America. The map below shows the location of the Ring of Fire and Earth's active volcanoes.

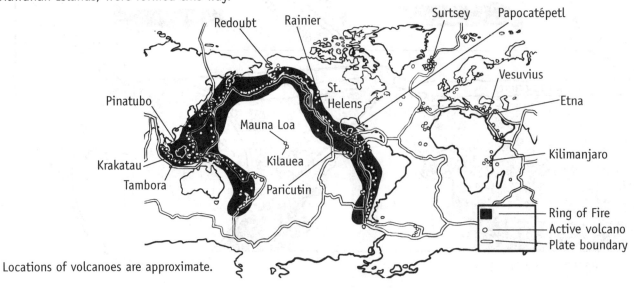

Locations of volcanoes are approximate.

www.harcourtschoolsupply.com
96
Lesson 9, Earth's History and Structure
Science 8, SV 9781419034367

Lesson 9

Darken the circle by the best answer.

1. Which of the following terms includes the other three terms?

   Ⓐ convergent boundary

   Ⓑ divergent boundary

   Ⓒ transform boundary

   Ⓓ plate tectonics

2. Which type of boundary forms when two continental plates collide?

   Ⓐ convergent boundary

   Ⓑ divergent boundary

   Ⓒ transform boundary

   Ⓓ oceanic-oceanic crust boundary

3. Which two structures make up the lithosphere?

   Ⓐ mantle and core

   Ⓑ crust and core

   Ⓒ crust and upper part of the mantle

   Ⓓ crust and asthenosphere

4. Mid-ocean ridges are created by a

   Ⓐ convergent boundary.

   Ⓑ divergent boundary.

   Ⓒ transform boundary.

   Ⓓ continental drift.

5. An opening in Earth through which magma can flow is called a(n)

   Ⓐ continental crust.

   Ⓑ oceanic crust.

   Ⓒ fault.

   Ⓓ volcano.

6. The San Andreas Fault is an example of a

   Ⓐ convergent boundary.

   Ⓑ divergent boundary.

   Ⓒ transform boundary.

   Ⓓ oceanic-oceanic crust boundary.

7. How does the asthenosphere differ from the lithosphere?

   _____

   _____

8. At a convergent boundary, oceanic crust always sinks beneath continental crust. Suggest a reason why this happens.

   _____

9. Would you expect to find a folded mountain range at a mid-ocean ridge? Explain your answer.

   _____

Lesson 9   Tectonic Plates

The following illustration shows the tectonic plates in certain parts of the world. The arrows indicate the direction in which each plate is moving. Notice that the arrows either point away from one another or toward one another. The numbers indicate how fast each plate is moving in centimeters per year. Use this illustration to answer the questions that follow.

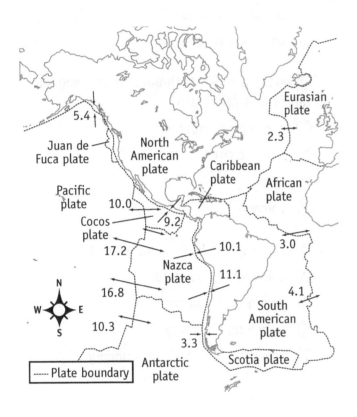

1. What type of boundary is found between the Eurasian plate and the North American plate? What may form along this boundary?

_____

_____

_____

_____

2. The Andes Mountains are located along the western coast of South America. How were these mountains formed?

_____

_____

_____

_____

_____

3. Where does a divergent boundary appear to be forming at the fastest rate? Explain your answer.

_____

_____

_____

_____

Lesson 9   Complete the Sentences

Use the following list of words to complete each sentence. Each word may be used only once.

asthenosphere	lithosphere	transform boundary
convergent boundary	magma	volcano
divergent boundary	mantle	
fault	tectonic plate	

1. Molten rock can rise up through a(n) _____, which is a large opening in Earth.

2. The _____ is the middle layer of Earth.

3. Two plates push together to form a(n) _____.

4. A(n) _____ is a break or crack in Earth's surface caused by movement.

5. Two plates slide across each other at a(n) _____.

6. The crust and the rigid upper part of the mantle make up the

   _____.

7. A(n) _____ is a large block of the crust and the rigid, outermost part of the mantle.

8. The soft layer of the mantle on which tectonic plates move is called the

   _____.

9. At a(n) _____, sea-floor spreading occurs to form new oceanic crust.

10. _____ that rises to the surface provides scientists with the opportunity to study Earth's interior.

Lesson 9   Seismic Waves

The speed of a seismic wave depends on the material through which it travels. The denser the material, the more quickly a seismic wave travels. Solids are usually denser than liquids. The following table shows the speeds of seismic waves through various layers of Earth. Use this table to answer the questions that follow.

Speed of Seismic Waves in Earth's Interior	
Physical layer	**Wave speed**
Lithosphere	7 to 8 km/s
Asthenosphere	7 to 11 km/s
Mesosphere	11 to 13 km/s
Outer core	8 to 10 km/s
Inner core	11 to 12 km/s

1. Which layer is the least dense? Explain your answer.

_____

_____

2. Which layer is the densest? Explain your answer.

_____

_____

3. Part of the core is solid, while the other part is liquid. Is the inner core or the outer core solid? Which part is liquid? Explain your answers.

_____

_____

4. If the lithosphere is 150 kilometers thick, how long would it take for seismic waves to travel through it?

_____

_____

Lesson 9   The Richter Scale

You may have heard of an earthquake being reported in terms of a Richter scale. In the 1930s, a scientist named Charles Richter developed a scale to measure the strength of earthquakes. Each unit on the Richter scale represents a magnitude difference of 10 times. For example, an earthquake with a magnitude of 4 on the Richter scale produces 10 times as much ground motion as an earthquake with a magnitude of 3. The following graph illustrates the relationship between magnitude and the height of waves on a seismogram that are generated by an earthquake. Use this graph to answer the questions that follow.

1. What is the magnitude of an earthquake if the maximum height of the seismogram waves is 40 mm?

_____

_____

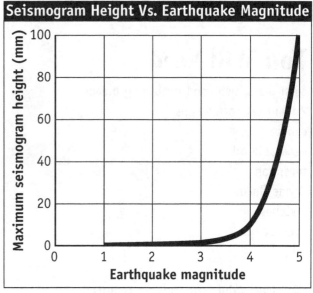

2. What is the maximum height of the seismogram waves generated by an earthquake with a magnitude of 4?

_____

_____

3. What is the difference in the maximum height of the seismogram waves between an earthquake with a magnitude of 4 and an earthquake of magnitude 5?

_____

4. Look at the shape of the curve on the graph. What conclusion can you draw based on this shape?

_____

_____

Lesson 9   Experiment: Convection Currents

Some scientists think tectonic plates move as a result of convection currents. If you have ever watched a pot of water boil, you have observed a convection current. A convection current is created by the transfer of thermal or heat energy as a liquid or gas circulates. Thermal energy from deep within Earth heats the rocks in the asthenosphere. The heat causes the rocks to expand. As they expand, the rocks become less dense and rise toward the surface. As they rise, the rocks cool, become more dense, and then sink. Some scientists think that this rising and sinking of the rocks cause tectonic plate motion. In the following experiment, you can see the movement caused by a convection current.

You Will Need

clear glass dish used for baking breads
2 identical coffee cups
candle
vegetable oil
teaspoon
thyme flakes
matches
cheesecloth
funnel

CAUTION: Adult supervision required.

Procedure

1. Set the baking dish so that each end rests on a coffee cup. Place the candle under the dish in the middle.

2. Fill the dish with the vegetable oil to a level about 1 inch below the top.

3. Add 2 teaspoons of thyme and stir thoroughly to distribute the flakes.

4. Light the candle and observe what happens to the flakes as the oil is heated. You do not have to heat the oil for long. Be sure to look both at the top and the side of the dish to observe the movement of the flakes.

5. Blow out the candle. Allow the oil to cool before pouring it through the cheesecloth to remove the thyme. You can then pour the oil back into its container.

Experiment: Convection Currents (cont'd.)

Results and Analysis

Use the illustration below to sketch how the flakes move in the baking dish.

Thermal Convection Experiment

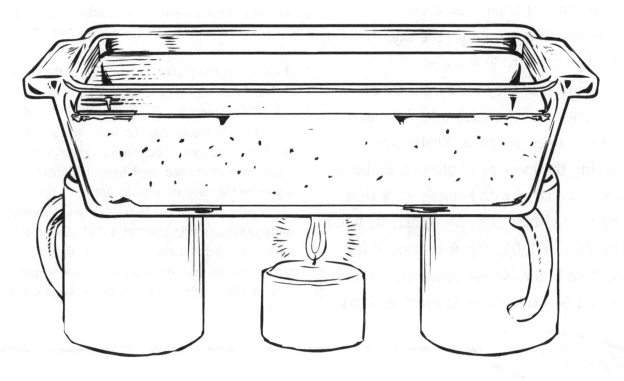

Conclusion

What conclusion can you draw based on your observations?

_____

_____

_____

_____

Lesson 10 Earth in the Solar System

During the 1500s, a Danish scientist named Tycho Brahe carefully observed the motion of the planets for more than 25 years. Brahe's observations provided much information, especially about the movement of Mars through the sky. His observations are truly amazing when considering that they were made before the invention of the telescope. A German scientist named Johannes Kepler was also observing the motions of planets. Brahe was so impressed with Kepler's work that Brahe invited him to be his assistant. When Brahe died in 1601, Kepler continued his work. Like Brahe, Kepler concentrated on Mars and eventually developed three laws

to describe the motion of all the planets around the sun.

Kepler's Three Laws

The path that Mars follows as it orbits the sun posed a problem for both Brahe and Kepler. At that time, scientists, including Brahe, thought that the shape of the orbits the planets follow around the sun were circles. Based on his observations and mathematical calculations, however, Brahe discovered that Mars did not travel around the sun in a circular orbit, like Earth appeared to do. Kepler's observation and calculations confirmed what Brahe had discovered. Kepler finally came up with an answer.

Kepler's solution led to his first law of planetary motion. Kepler's first law states that planets orbit the sun in an elongated circle called an ellipse. An ellipse can be considered a flattened circle. An **ellipse** is more precisely defined as a closed curve in which the

Key Terms

ellipse—a closed curve in which the sum of the distances from the edge of the curve to two points inside the curve is always the same

revolution—a complete trip of a body along its orbit around another body

astronomical unit (AU)—the average distance between the sun and Earth, or approximately 95 million miles

photosphere—the visible surface of the sun

sunspot—an area of gases on the sun that is cooler than the gases around them

solar flare—a region of extremely high temperature and brightness that develops on the sun's surface and results in an explosion

rotation—the spinning of an object on its axis

phase—a difference in the appearance of an object in space caused by changes in sunlit areas

eclipse—an event that occurs when the shadow of one celestial body falls on another celestial body

solar eclipse—an event that occurs when the moon comes between Earth and the sun

lunar eclipse—an event that occurs when Earth comes between the sun and the moon

sum of the distances from the edge of the curve to two points inside the curve is always the same. Each point inside the ellipse is called a focus, as shown in the following illustration.

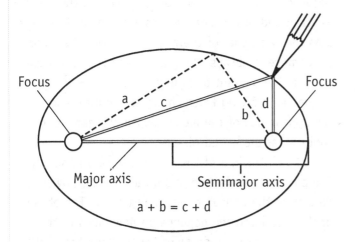

Notice in the figure above that the maximum length of an ellipse is called its *major axis*. Half this distance is its *semimajor axis*. In an elliptical orbit, the semimajor axis represents the average distance that a planet is from the sun. The semimajor axis of Earth is about 95 million miles, which is its average distance from the sun over the course of a year.

Kepler's second law states that a planet moves faster when it is closer to the sun and slower when it is farther away from the sun. The illustration below shows that, for equal amounts of time, a planet sweeps out the same area as it travels around the sun in an ellipse.

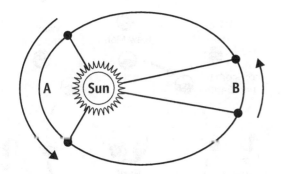

Kepler's third law explains the relationship between a planet's semimajor axis and its period of revolution. A **revolution** represents one complete trip of a planet along its orbit around the sun. By knowing how long it took for a planet to orbit the sun, Kepler was able to calculate its semimajor axis, or its average distance from the sun.

The unit for a planet's semimajor axis is the **astronomical unit** (**AU**). One AU is the average distance between the sun and Earth, or approximately 95 million miles. Kepler determined that Mars's period of revolution is 1.88 Earth years. Based on this value, Kepler calculated Mars's semimajor axis to be 1.5 AU. Although Kepler did not know how many miles 1.5 AU represented, he did know that Mars was 1.5 times farther than Earth from the sun. In this way, Kepler also figured out that Mercury was a third as far from the sun as Earth was. In other words, Kepler's third law allowed him to calculate the relative distances of the planets from the center of our universe—the sun.

The Sun

The sun is the dominant object in our solar system because it makes up more than 99 percent of all the solar system's mass. The sun is also the dominant object because it provides the energy for all life on Earth, the only planet where living things are known to exist.

The sun generates energy by a process called nuclear fusion. You learned in Lesson 3 that nuclear fusion is the process by which two smaller atomic nuclei combine to form a larger nucleus, releasing a tremendous amount of energy. In the sun, four hydrogen nuclei fuse to form a single nucleus of helium. As a result of each fusion, an extremely small amount of mass is changed into energy. You also learned in Lesson 3 that Einstein showed that this conversion produces a tremendous amount of energy based on his famous formula, $E = mc^2$.

The fusion reactions occur in the center, or core, of the sun. Taking millions of years, the energy released in the core finally reaches the surface of the sun, known as the **photosphere**. The energy leaves the photosphere as light, which takes only 8.3 minutes to travel some 95 million miles through space to reach Earth.

In addition to light, nuclear fusion also produces a tremendous amount of heat. As a result, the gases that make up the sun get extremely hot. At times, some areas of the photosphere are hotter than others. The cooler gases in the photosphere do not give off as much light as the hotter gases. These cooler gases look darker when observed from Earth. These darker areas are called **sunspots**. The Italian scientist Galileo Galilei first observed sunspots in the early 1600s.

Since Galileo's observations, scientists have discovered that sunspot activity follows a regular cycle. Every 11 years, sunspot activity reaches a peak and then decreases. The graph below shows sunspot activity for a 20-year period beginning in 1980.

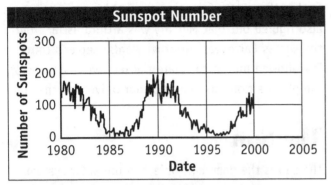

Sometimes, the areas surrounding sunspots combine to form one large, extremely hot region known as a solar flare. A **solar flare** is a region of extremely high temperature and brightness that develops on the sun's surface and results in an explosion. The explosion sends solar particles far out into space where they eventually reach Earth's atmosphere. Here the solar particles can disrupt television, radio, and telephone communications. These particles can also cause electrical problems for homes and businesses. Scientists are trying to find ways to predict when solar flares will occur to give warning of the possible consequences.

The Moon

All the planets orbit the sun. However, some of the planets have bodies that orbit them. These bodies are moons. Mercury and Venus are the only two planets that do not have a moon.

The Apollo missions to Earth's moon provided scientists with much of what we know about this body. The lunar rocks were found to be about 4.6 billion years old and to be similar to rocks on Earth. These discoveries support the theory that the moon was formed about the same time as Earth. A large object, about the size of Mars, is thought to have collided with Earth. This collision sent a large part of Earth into space where it formed the moon.

The moon revolves in a counterclockwise direction around Earth once every 27 days and 7 hours. The moon's period of rotation is 27 days, 9 hours. A **rotation** is the spinning of an object on its axis. Because the moon's period of revolution is the same as its period of rotation, an observer on Earth always sees the same side of the moon. However, the moon's appearance is always changing. These changes occur because the amount of sunlight that strikes the side of the moon facing Earth changes. The differences in the appearance of the moon caused by changes in sunlit areas are called **phases**.

Like Earth, half of the moon is always in sunlight. The positions of the sun, moon, and Earth, however, determine the phase of the moon we see. The phase of the moon you see depends on how much of the sunlit side of the moon faces Earth. When the sunlit fraction we see is getting larger, the moon is said to be waxing. When the sunlit fraction is getting smaller, the moon is waning. The illustration below shows the various phases of the waxing and waning moon with the sun shining from the top.

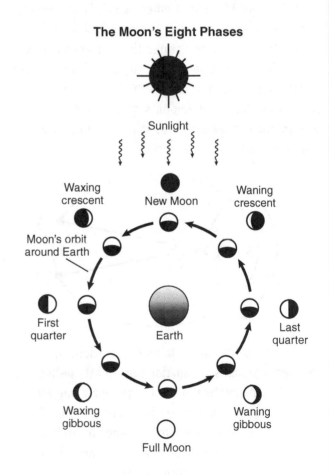

The Moon's Eight Phases

Eclipses

The sun, moon, and Earth sometimes line up to create eclipses. An **eclipse** occurs when the shadow of one celestial body falls on another. A **solar eclipse** occurs when the moon comes between Earth and the sun. As a result, the shadow of the moon falls on part of Earth. Like the orbits of the planets, the moon's orbit is elliptical. When the moon is closer to Earth, the moon completely covers the sun. When the moon is farther from Earth, a tiny ring of the sun shows around the moon's outer edge.

A **lunar eclipse** occurs when Earth comes between the sun and the moon. As a result, the shadow of Earth falls on the moon. If you look at the phases of the moon on page 106, you would think that a solar eclipse should occur during every new moon and that a lunar eclipse should occur during every full moon. However, the moon's orbit is slightly tilted with respect to Earth's orbit. This tilt is enough to place Earth out of the moon's shadow for most new moons and place the moon out of Earth's shadow for most full moons.

Lesson 10   Review

Darken the circle by the best answer.

1. Earth completes one rotation
   - Ⓐ about once a year.
   - Ⓑ about every 24 hours.
   - Ⓒ only during a full moon.
   - Ⓓ by orbiting the sun.

2. The average distance between a planet and the sun is represented by
   - Ⓐ 1 AU.
   - Ⓑ the major axis of its elliptical orbit.
   - Ⓒ the semimajor axis of its elliptical orbit.
   - Ⓓ twice the distance between Earth and the sun.

3. During a solar eclipse,
   - Ⓐ the sun's shadow falls on Earth.
   - Ⓑ Earth's shadow falls on the sun.
   - Ⓒ Earth's shadow falls on the moon.
   - Ⓓ the moon's shadow falls on Earth.

4. Which of the following is responsible for periodic disruptions in Earth's communication systems?
   - Ⓐ solar flares
   - Ⓑ solar eclipses
   - Ⓒ new moons
   - Ⓓ Earth's rotation

5. Kepler's third law
   - Ⓐ states that planets travel in elliptical orbits.
   - Ⓑ states that planets travel faster when they are closer to the sun.
   - Ⓒ explains the relationship between a planet's period of rotation and its semimajor axis.
   - Ⓓ explains the relationship between a planet's period of revolution and its semimajor axis.

6. Only one side of the moon is always visible to Earth because the moon
   - Ⓐ revolves but does not rotate.
   - Ⓑ rotates but does not revolve.
   - Ⓒ has the same period of rotation as its period of revolution.
   - Ⓓ has an axis that is slightly tilted with respect to Earth's axis.

7. Is the side of the moon that we do not see from Earth always dark? Explain your answer.

   _____

   _____

   _____

8. If a planet has a semimajor axis of 5.74 AU, what information does this provide about this planet in relation to Earth?

   _____

   _____

Lesson 10

The Moon's Orbit

The diagram below models the moon's orbit around Earth. Use this diagram to answer the questions that follow.

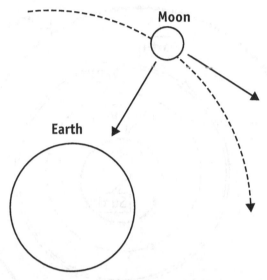

1. What is represented by the arrow pointing from the moon toward Earth?

   Ⓐ inertia

   Ⓑ gravitational attraction

   Ⓒ acceleration

   Ⓓ Kepler's first law of motion

2. The moon would follow the path indicated by the arrow pointing into space as a result of

   Ⓐ inertia.

   Ⓑ gravitational attraction.

   Ⓒ velocity.

   Ⓓ Kepler's third law of motion.

3. Based on this diagram, a valid conclusion would be that

   Ⓐ the moon moves in three different directions depending on its speed.

   Ⓑ Kepler's first law of motion does not apply to the moon.

   Ⓒ the moon is moving away from Earth.

   Ⓓ the moon's orbit depends on two factors represented by the solid arrows.

4. What would happen to gravitational attraction if the moon had a larger mass?

   Ⓐ It would increase.

   Ⓑ It would stay the same.

   Ⓒ It would decrease.

   Ⓓ The moon would start to move away from Earth.

5. The moon would move toward Earth if the moon

   Ⓐ underwent an increase in acceleration.

   Ⓑ rotated more slowly.

   Ⓒ stopped revolving.

   Ⓓ revolved around Earth in the opposite direction.

Lesson 10

Kepler's Laws

The diagram below shows the orbits of the four planets closest to the sun. Use this diagram to answer the questions that follow.

1. Which planet best demonstrates Kepler's first law of motion? Explain your answer.

_____

_____

_____

_____

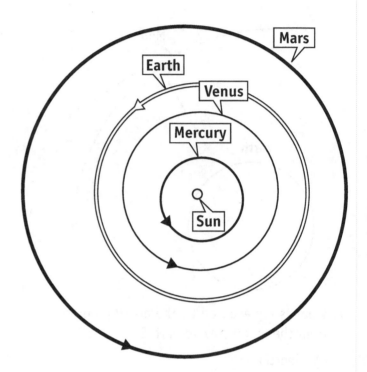

2. Assume that the orbits in this diagram are superimposed on the face of a clock. At what time on the clock will Mars be traveling the fastest according to Kepler's second law of motion? Explain your answer.

_____

_____

_____

3. According to Kepler's third law of motion, which planet has the shortest semimajor axis? Explain your answer.

_____

_____

_____

Lesson 10   Squeeze Gently

Read the following passage and then answer the questions.

Suppose you place a rubber ball between your thumb and forefinger and squeeze gently. The ball would flatten a little bit at the top and bottom and bulge slightly around the middle. This is similar to the shape of the moon. The fact that the moon is slightly squashed is not surprising. Like all the planets, the moon rotates on its axis. This spinning motion creates a force. This is a centrifugal force that would have spun out magma as the moon was forming. This magma would have collected and hardened along the moon's equator, which is where it bulges today.

However, scientists were puzzled because the moon's bulge is greater than expected. Scientists can calculate how much centrifugal force is generated by the moon's mass that rotates every 27 days and 7 hours. The strength of this centrifugal force is not enough to explain a 2.5-mile bulge. In effect, the moon was too flat.

Scientists have recently proposed an answer to this puzzle about the moon. During the 1970s, the Apollo astronauts left mirrors on the moon. Since then, laser beams have been bounced off these mirrors, showing that each year the moon is moving 1.5 inches farther from Earth. Scientists believe that at one time the moon was much closer to Earth, perhaps just 16,000 miles away. Today, the moon is roughly 238,000 miles from Earth.

Not only was the moon closer, it was also rotating faster. Scientists suggest that in its early history, the moon had a 3:2 resonance, which means that it rotated three times for every two revolutions. Today, the moon has a 1:1 resonance. A more rapid spin could explain why the moon developed such a large bulge around its equator when it formed. The squeeze might have been stronger than it was first thought.

1. What caused the "squeeze" that flattened the moon?
   - Ⓐ resonance
   - Ⓑ laser beams being bounced off mirrors
   - Ⓒ centrifugal force
   - Ⓓ Earth

2. A 1:1 resonance means that the moon
   - Ⓐ revolves around Earth.
   - Ⓑ completes one rotation for every revolution.
   - Ⓒ rotates every 27 days and 7 hours.
   - Ⓓ is 238,000 miles from Earth.

3. How much farther from Earth will the moon be in 1000 years?
   - Ⓐ 1.5 inches
   - Ⓑ 15 inches
   - Ⓒ 150 inches
   - Ⓓ 1500 inches

Lesson 10   The Sun

The graph below shows the relationship between the age of a star, such as our sun, and its mass. Use this graph to answer the questions that follow.

1. What conclusion can you draw from this graph about the relationship between a star's mass and its age?

   _____

   _____

   _____

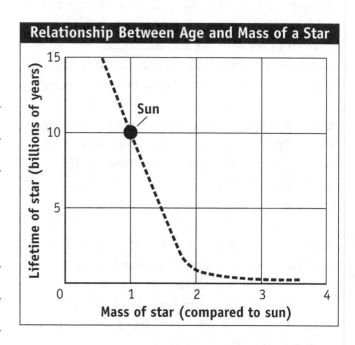

2. If the sun were formed 4.6 billion years ago, how much longer is the sun expected to exist?

   _____

   _____

   _____

The graph below shows the number of sunspots that have occurred between the time Galileo first spotted them and 1960. Use this graph to answer the questions that follow.

3. Scientists have linked increased sunspot activity with periods on Earth of high temperatures. When did Earth experience a period known as the "Little Ice Age"? Explain your answer.

   _____

   _____

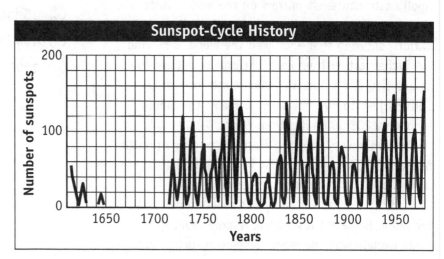

4. When did Earth likely experience the warmest temperatures? Explain your answer.

   _____

   _____

Lesson 10

Experiment: Calculating the Distance to the Sun

You read that Tycho Brahe made his observations about the planets before the telescope was invented. He was not the first to study celestial bodies without the help of a telescope. Eratosthenes was a Greek scholar who lived between 276 and 194 BC and worked in Cyrene and Alexandria. Eratosthenes is remembered for a simple technique that enabled him to compute the first reliable determination of the true size of Earth. Eratosthenes determined that Earth's circumference was about 25,000 miles, a number which is remarkably close to the actual value. In the following experiment, you will use a simple technique to calculate how far the sun is from Earth.

You Will Need

helper
scissors
ruler
poster board
aluminum foil
tape
thumbtack
window that faces the sun
yardstick
index card
calculator

Procedure

1. Cut a 2-inch × 2-inch square in the middle of the poster board.

2. Cut a 3-inch × 3-inch piece of aluminum foil. Tape the aluminum foil over the square you cut in the poster board.

3. Use a thumbtack to prick a tiny hole in the center of the aluminum foil.

4. Tape the poster board to the inside of the window. Sunlight must shine directly through the tiny hole in the aluminum foil and into the room. Be certain never to look through the pinhole at the sun!

5. Darken the room.

Experiment: Calculating the Distance to the Sun (cont'd.)

6. Place one end of the yardstick against the window beneath the foil square. Use one hand to steady the yardstick.

7. Use your other hand to hold the index card close to the pinhole in the aluminum foil. A circular image of the sun should appear on the index card.

8. Slide the card along the yardstick away from the aluminum foil until the sun's image is large enough to measure. Be sure that the end of the yardstick is still against the aluminum foil and the card is resting on the yardstick.

9. Have your helper use the ruler to measure the diameter of the sun's image on the card. Measure the diameter to the nearest $\frac{1}{16}$ of an inch. Also record the distance between the card and the aluminum foil. You are now ready to calculate the distance between the sun and Earth.

Results and Analysis

1. Calculate the distance between the sun and Earth by using the following formula. In addition to the two values you recorded, you will need the sun's diameter, which is 54,800,000,000 inches.

$$\text{distance} = \text{sun's diameter} \times \frac{\text{distance between foil and card}}{\text{diameter of sun's image}}$$

2. The sun is about 93 million miles from Earth. How close is your calculation to this figure? You must convert your answer in inches from step 1 to miles. First, convert inches to feet, and then convert feet to miles using the following conversion factors.

12 inches = 1 foot   5280 feet = 1 mile

Conclusion

What conclusion can you draw based upon your observations?

_____

_____

_____

Science Fair Projects

Although it is at the end of the lesson, each experiment in this book should be the beginning for learning something about science. For example, you may have done the experiment titled *Extracting DNA* and isolated the DNA from split peas. But you can also experiment with other foods such as spinach, broccoli, chicken liver, and strawberries. You can also try to develop your own method to extract DNA by testing various detergents to see if one works best. Check to see if something works better than meat tenderizer to break down the proteins. In other words, you should be creative, like any good scientist.

Designing an Experiment

If you design your own experiment, be sure that you do so safely and correctly. You must carry out all your work with the supervision of an adult, either your parent or teacher. The adult must help with any procedure that involves a risk. For example, the experiment may require the use of a sharp knife or hot stove. The adult should perform these steps. In addition, you must have an adult review the materials you will use and the procedure you will follow *before* you begin any experiment or science fair project.

Also be sure that your experiment has been designed correctly. Whenever a scientist designs an experiment, he or she always includes a control. A control is set up so that only one factor or variable is present in the experiment. A variable is anything that changes.

For example, suppose you do a project that involves planting seeds in flower pots to investigate if plants compete for space as they grow. You decide to plant 3 seeds in half the pots, and 15 seeds in the other half. All the pots must be treated in the same way. They must contain the same amount of potting soil, and they must receive the same amount of light and water. If the plants grow taller in the pots with only 3 seeds, then you can conclude that competition for space limited the growth in the other pots. In this experiment, the only variable was the number of seeds planted in the pots. No other factor that could affect the result was introduced into the experiment.

Choosing a Project

Any experiment in this book can serve as the basis for a science fair project. Usually, doing a science fair project is a bit more involved than carrying out an experiment. Rather than use an experiment in this book as your starting point, you may want to pick your own topic to investigate. If you do, you will have to do some research to learn something about the topic. This research can involve checking the Internet, reading books, and talking to teachers and scientists.

A good place to begin is to think about what you like. For example, if you like building models, then you may want to build a model that explains a scientific principle or concept. Pennies were used as a model of a radioactive substance in Lesson 3 to explain the concepts of nuclear fission and half-life. You can build a model to show what happens as a result of nuclear fusion.

Deciding what to do for a science fair project is often the hardest part of the project. If you have trouble choosing a project, then here are some ideas from each lesson in this book. These ideas will get you started. However, you will have to obtain more information to carry out the project. You can get this information from the Internet, the library, or your teachers. You can also check companies that sell to individuals for items that can help you with your project.

Lesson 1 Properties and Changes of Properties in Matter

- **Solubility Curves**—The amount of a substance that dissolves in water depends on temperature. The solubility of most substances increases as the temperature increases. Construct solubility curves for various substances by determining how much of each substance dissolves at various temperatures. Include substances whose solubility decreases with an increase in temperature. Provide an explanation as to why these substances behave differently.

- **Spontaneous Reactions**—Many chemical reactions occur spontaneously when the reactants are mixed. Other chemical reactions, however, do not occur spontaneously. Demonstrate examples of each type of reaction. Explain what is required for a chemical reaction to take place spontaneously. You will need to research concepts such as entropy, enthalpy, and Gibbs free energy.

- **Colligative Property**—This is a physical property that is affected by how much of a substance is added rather than on the type of substance that is added. Both the freezing point depression and the boiling point elevation of a liquid are examples of colligative properties. Demonstrate a colligative property and relate its importance in some practical application. For example, the antifreeze added to a car's radiator makes use of a colligative property.

Lesson 2 Motions and Forces

- **Magic Tricks**—Some magic tricks can be performed because of Newton's first law of motion. For example, you may have seen someone remove a tablecloth while leaving the dishes and glasses undisturbed on the table. Find out what other magic tricks can be performed because of Newton's law. Explain how inertia is involved in each trick.

- **Gravity**—Determine the acceleration of an object due to gravity using Newton's second law of motion. This project can be done with a toy cart on wheels, long table, pulley with mounting clamps, string, timer, and weights. Explain the relationship between force, mass, and acceleration.

- **Bats and Balls**—Newton's third law of motion explains what happens when a bat makes contact with a baseball thrown by a pitcher. Hitting a home run depends on several factors, including whether the ball is hit on the "sweet spot" of the bat. Conduct a project to demonstrate the location of a bat's "sweet spot" and how it affects the action-reaction pair.

Lesson 3 Transfer of Energy

- **Chemical Energy**—Calculate the chemical energy that is stored in a food such as a peanut or potato chip. You will have to build a calorimeter and measure the temperature change of a sample of water as the food burns. Getting the food to start burning is the most difficult part. You may want to build a combustion chamber as part of your calorimeter so that the food sample starts burning more easily. Compare the values you obtain to those printed on the food product. Explain any differences between these values.

- **Nuclear Power**—Build a model of a nuclear power plant. Explain the function of each part. Include calculations to show how much energy can be generated by nuclear fission, using Einstein's equation $E = mc^2$. Research the current status of nuclear power in the United States and present your findings.

- **Catalysts**—A catalyst is a substance that speeds up the rate of a chemical reaction by lowering the activation energy. Demonstrate the effect of a catalyst. You can also explore the function of enzymes, which are catalysts found in living things. Include information about how enzymes are thought to function. Also investigate how enzymes are affected by changes in temperature and pH.

Lesson 4 Structure and Function in Living Systems

- **Dialysis**—People whose kidneys are not functioning normally may have to be placed on a dialysis machine. Use dialysis tubing to demonstrate how this machine purifies the blood. Explain what factors affect the ability of substances to pass through dialysis tubing. Include information about how a dialysis machine functions.

- **Plant Hormones**—Hormones play an important role in plant responses to changes in their environment. These hormones include auxins, which regulate plant growth; gibberillins, which stimulate cell division; and ethylene, which promotes fruit ripening. Design a project that demonstrates how a plant hormone affects its development. Include current information about the hormone, including any practical applications.

- **Reflexes**—Design a project that tests whether a certain reflex behavior operates the same in all people. For example, check if eighth-grade boys and eighth-grade girls have the same reaction times in a reflex behavior. A simple procedure is to measure the time it takes to stop a yardstick from falling. Check several reflex behaviors to see if reaction time is always faster in one group despite the behavior that is performed. Find out how reaction time can be improved.

Lesson 5 Reproduction and Heredity

- **DNA**—Extract the DNA from peas, spinach, broccoli, and chicken liver. Both a detergent to break open the cells and a chemical substance to break down proteins are required. First, use a procedure you find by researching the Internet. Then, try to improve on the procedure so that fewer steps are needed or more DNA is extracted from the same amount of sample material.
- **The Double Helix**—Make a model of DNA just like Watson and Crick did. Show how DNA is copied in a process called replication. Demonstrate how changing just one base in your DNA model affects the process of replication and the protein that is synthesized.
- **DNA Fingerprinting**—The use of DNA fingerprinting to convict criminals and establish blood relationships has generated much publicity. Explain the scientific basis of how such a fingerprint is prepared and analyzed. To obtain information, contact a laboratory where such a procedure is done. Provide examples to show how DNA fingerprints have been used.

Lesson 6 Regulation and Behavior

- **Taste**—Find out where the specialized nerve cells for sweetness, sourness, saltiness, and bitterness

are located on the tongue. Determine if they are located in the same general area in different people. You will have to place a sweet, sour, salty, and bitter sample on different parts of the tongue. Check to see how a taste can be changed. For example, repeat the experiment after your subject brushes his or her teeth with toothpaste that contains sodium lauryl sulfate.

- **Optical Illusions**—Use a Benham disk to demonstrate that a person will see black-and-white images in color. Try making a variety of Benham disks to see what colors people see. Include information about what scientists think is happening when people interpret black-and-white images in color. Check out other "optical illusions" and explain how these images "fool" the brain.
- **Homeostasis**—Use an organism known as a paramecium to demonstrate how its contractile vacuole maintains homeostasis. The rate at which the vacuole expels water will change depending on the water concentration in its environment. Time how many times the vacuole fills and then expels water under different conditions. This project will require patient observations with a microscope.

Lesson 7 Populations and Ecosystems

- **Respiration**—Build a respirometer to measure the respiration rate of an organism. You can use either a small animal such as cricket or plants such as peas. Determine what factors affect the rate of respiration. Obtain information on the differences between aerobic and anaerobic respiration.
- **Photosynthesis**—Determine how temperature and light intensity affect the amount of oxygen released by plants during photosynthesis. You can use a freshwater plant called elodea that gives off oxygen bubbles while it carries out photosynthesis. Try to develop a device that measures the volume of oxygen that is produced under different conditions.
- **Eutrophication**—Organisms need nutrients, such as nitrogen, to survive. However, too many nutrients can cause problems. The process by which an ecosystem receives too many nutrients,

such as nitrates, is called eutrophication. Demonstrate the effect of eutrophication by adding fertilizer to pond water and see how the organisms are affected.

Lesson 8 Diversity and Adaptations of Organisms

- **Fossils**—Make your own fossil prints from specimens such as seashells and chicken bones. Demonstrate the difference between a cast and a mold. Prepare your own molds and casts. Include information on how the age of a fossil is determined. Dating fossils depends on the half-life of a radioactive substance.
- **Cladograms**—The evolutionary history of different species is sometimes illustrated with a cladogram. Prepare one or more cladograms to show evolutionary relationships. You will have to check the various styles that are used to draw a cladogram. Be sure to use one that is easy to follow.
- **Natural Selection**—Charles Darwin developed the theory of natural selection to explain how evolution occurs. You can either report on an example of natural selection such as industrial melanism in the peppered moth or carry out experiments showing how resistance to antibiotics can evolve in bacteria. You will have to learn how to culture bacteria and take special precautions to prevent any direct contact with the bacteria. Be sure to work under adult supervision at all times.

Lesson 9 Earth's History and Structure

- **Earthquakes**—Design a model to show what features help a building withstand an earthquake. Research the Internet for information on how major cities such as Los Angeles and Tokyo have developed building codes to minimize damage from earthquakes. Test your model by placing it on a tray of gelatin and shaking it.
- **Seismic Waves**—Use seismographs to explain the difference between P waves and S waves. Explain how seismologists use the S–P time method to find an earthquake's epicenter. Include information on the Richter scale and the modified Mercalli Intensity Scale.
- **Mountains**—Use models to describe how tectonic plate movements form folded mountains, fault-block mountains, and volcanic mountains. Include information about the type of boundary where these mountains form and the three stages involved in mountain building.

Lesson 10 Earth in the Solar System

- **Measuring Earth's Circumference**—Repeat Eratosthenes's experiment in which he calculated Earth's circumference. You will need someone as far north or south as possible of your location to make the same measurements. With an adult, use the Internet to try to find someone your age who would be willing to cooperate.
- **Telescope**—This device has provided much information about our solar system. Research the Internet for information on how to build a simple telescope. Use it to make observations of objects in the sky. Prepare a report summarizing your observations.
- **Projectile Motion**—The planets exhibit projectile motion, which is the curved path an object follows. Projectile motion has two components. One is horizontal motion due to the object's velocity. The other component is vertical motion due to gravity. Show how projectile motion affects where a person must aim when throwing or shooting an object.

Glossary

abiotic factor—a nonliving component in the environment (p. 72)

acceleration—a change in velocity (p. 18)

activation energy—the smallest amount of energy required to start a chemical reaction (p. 29)

adaptation—a feature that increases an organism's chances to survive and reproduce (p. 83)

artificial selection—the human practice of breeding plants or animals that have certain desirable traits; also known as selective breeding (p. 83)

asthenosphere—the molten layer of the mantle on which tectonic plates move (p. 93)

astronomical unit (AU)—the average distance between the sun and Earth, or approximately 95 million miles (p. 104)

atom—the basic building block of matter (p. 7)

behavior—an action or series of actions that an animal performs in response to a stimulus (p. 62)

biodiversity—the variety and complexity of life that exists on Earth (p. 83)

biotic factor—a living component in the environment (p. 72)

boiling point—the temperature at which a liquid boils to form a gas (p. 7)

carrying capacity—the largest population that an environment can support at any given time (p. 72)

cell—the smallest unit of an organism that can perform all life processes (p. 40)

central nervous system—the brain and spinal cord (p. 40)

cerebellum—the part of the brain that controls muscle coordination (p. 40)

cerebrum—the part of the brain that gathers, interprets, and responds to information (p. 40)

chemical change—a change that results in the change of the identity of a substance (p. 7)

chemical energy—the energy of a substance that changes as its atoms are rearranged (p. 29)

chemical equation—a shorthand method to show what happens during a chemical reaction (p. 7)

chemical formula—a shorthand way to use chemical symbols and numbers to represent a substance (p. 7)

chemical property—a property that describes matter based on its ability to change into new matter that has different properties (p. 7)

chemical reaction—a process in which one or more substances change to make one or more new substances (p. 7)

chromosome—the cell structure that stores the hereditary information (p. 51)

cochlea—a fluid-filled structure that makes up part of the inner ear (p. 62)

combustion—the burning of a substance such as wood or coal (p. 72)

community—the different populations that live in the same place (p. 72)

condensation—the change of a substance from a gas to a liquid (p. 72)

continental drift—the theory that the continents once formed a single landmass (p. 93)

convergent boundary—the location where two tectonic plates push into one another (p. 93)

core—the central part of Earth below the mantle (p. 93)

crust—the solid outermost layer of Earth (p. 93)

decomposition—the breakdown of substances into simpler substances (p. 72)

density—the ratio of the mass of a substance to the volume of the substance (p. 7)

deoxyribonucleic acid (DNA)—the chemical substance in a chromosome that contains the hereditary information (p. 51)

divergent boundary—the location where two tectonic plates move away from one another (p. 93)

earthquake—the shaking of Earth's surface (p. 93)

eclipse—an event that occurs when the shadow of one celestial body falls on another celestial body (p. 104)

ecosystem—all the organisms within a community and the nonliving things with which they interact (p. 72)

electron—a particle that orbits the nucleus of an atom (p. 29)

ellipse—a closed curve in which the sum of the distances from the edge of the curve to two points inside the curve is always the same (p. 104)

endocrine system—the system that controls body functions by using chemicals (p. 40)

endothermic reaction—a chemical reaction that absorbs energy (p. 7)

energy—the ability to do work (p. 29)

evaporation—the change of a substance from a liquid to a gas (p. 72)

evolution—the gradual change in a species over time (p. 83)

exothermic reaction—a chemical reaction that releases energy (p. 7)

fallopian tube—a tube that leads from the ovary to the uterus (p. 40)

fault—a break or crack in Earth's surface along which movement has occurred (p. 93)

force—a push or a pull (p. 18)

fossil—the remains or physical evidence of an organism that has been preserved by natural processes (p. 83)

friction—the force that opposes motion between two surfaces that are in contact (p. 18)

gene—a set of instructions stored on a chromosome that determines a particular trait (p. 51)

genetic engineering—the manipulation of genes for practical purposes (p. 51)

genome—the complete set of an organism's DNA (p. 51)

gravity—the force of attraction between two objects that is due to their masses (p. 18)

heredity—the passing of traits from parents to offspring (p. 51)

homeostasis—the maintenance of a constant internal environment despite changes in the external environment (p. 62)

hormone—a substance made in one cell or tissue that causes a change in another cell or tissue (p. 40)

inertia—the tendency of an object to resist a change in motion (p. 18)

kidney—the organ that filters wastes from the blood and produces urine (p. 40)

law of conservation of energy—the law that states that energy cannot be either created or destroyed (p. 29)

law of conservation of mass—the law that states that mass cannot be created or destroyed during ordinary physical and chemical changes (p. 7)

limiting factor—any natural resource that limits the size of a population (p. 72)

lithosphere—the outermost rigid layer of Earth made of the crust and the solid upper part of the mantle (p. 93)

lunar eclipse—an event that occurs when Earth comes between the sun and the moon (p. 104)

magma—hot, liquid rock (p. 93)

mantle—the layer between Earth's crust and core (p. 93)

mass—the amount of matter in an object (p. 7)

matter—anything that has both volume and mass (p. 7)

medulla—the part of the brain that controls involuntary processes (p. 40)

melting point—the temperature at which a solid melts to form a liquid (p. 7)

menstrual cycle—the 28-day cycle that involves changes in the female reproductive system (p. 40)

motion—the change in position of an object over time with respect to a reference point (p. 18)

mutation—a change in a gene or DNA (p. 51)

natural selection—the process by which evolution is thought to occur (p. 83)

nephron—the unit in the kidney that filters blood (p. 40)

neutron—a particle that makes up part of the nucleus of an atom (p. 29)

newton—the unit for force (p. 18)

Newton's first law of motion—the law that states that an object at rest remains at rest and that an object in motion remains in motion at constant speed and in a straight line unless a force causes it to change speed or direction (p. 18)

Newton's second law of motion—the law that states that the overall force on an object is equal to the mass of the object multiplied by the acceleration of the object (p. 18)

Newton's third law of motion—the law that states that whenever one object exerts a force on a second object, the second object exerts an equal and opposite force on the first object (p. 18)

nitrogen fixation—the process in which bacteria change nitrogen gas into a form plants can use (p. 72)

nuclear chain reaction—a continuous series of nuclear reactions (p. 29)

nuclear fission—the process by which a nucleus splits into two smaller nuclei, releasing a tremendous amount of energy (p. 29)

nuclear fusion—the process by which two smaller atomic nuclei combine to form a larger nucleus, releasing a tremendous amount of energy (p. 29)

nuclear reaction—a reaction involving the nucleus of an atom (p. 29)

nucleus—the central part of an atom (p. 29)

olfactory cell—a nerve cell that detects chemical substances in the air (p. 62)

organ—a group of tissues that work together for a specific job (p. 40)

organ system—a group of organs that work together for a specific job (p. 40)

organism—a living thing (p. 40)

ovary—the female reproductive organ where eggs are produced (p. 40)

papilla—a tiny bump on the tongue that may contain a taste bud (p. 62)

peripheral nervous system—the parts of the nervous system other than the brain and spinal cord (p. 40)

phase—a difference in the appearance of an object in space caused by changes in sunlit areas (p. 104)

photoreceptor—a specialized cell in the retina that detects light and then sends signals to the brain (p. 62)

photosphere—the visible surface of the sun (p. 104)

photosynthesis—the process in which plants use light energy to change carbon dioxide and water into sugars and oxygen (p. 72)

physical change—a change that does not change the identity of a substance (p. 7)

physical property—a property of matter that can be observed or measured without changing the matter's identity (p. 7)

plate tectonics—the theory that Earth's lithosphere is divided into tectonic plates that can move around on top of the asthenosphere (p. 93)

population—all the members of the same species that live in the same place (p. 72)

precipitation—any form of water that falls to Earth from the clouds (p. 72)

product—the substance that is made during a chemical reaction (p. 7)

proton—a particle that makes up part of the nucleus of an atom (p. 29)

reactant—a substance that reacts with another substance in a chemical reaction (p. 7)

reactivity—the ability of one substance to interact chemically with another substance (p. 7)

recombinant DNA—the combination of DNA from two or more sources (p. 51)

reflex—an involuntary response that does not involve the brain (p. 40)

respiration—the process of using oxygen to break down sugars and release energy (p. 72)

retina—the inner layer of specialized cells found at the back of the eye (p. 62)

revolution—a complete trip of a body along its orbit around another body (p. 104)

ribonucleic acid (RNA)—the chemical substance that plays a role in the production of proteins (p. 51)

rotation—the spinning of an object on its axis (p. 104)

sea-floor spreading—the process by which new oceanic lithosphere forms as magma rises from the mantle and solidifies (p. 93)

seismic wave—a wave of energy that travels through Earth and away from an earthquake in all directions (p. 93)

sensory organ—an organ that is specialized to detect a stimulus (p. 62)

solar eclipse—an event that occurs when the moon comes between Earth and the sun (p. 104)

solar flare—a region of extremely high temperature and brightness that develops on the sun's surface and results in an explosion (p. 104)

solubility—the ability of one substance to dissolve in another substance (p. 7)

solution—a mixture made by dissolving one substance in another substance (p. 7)

speciation—the formation of a new species as a result of evolution (p. 83)

species—a group of organisms that have common features and can mate to produce fertile offspring (p. 72)

speed—the distance traveled by an object divided by the time taken to travel that distance (p. 18)

stimulus—anything that causes a response (p. 62)

sunspot—an area of gases on the sun that is cooler than the gases around them (p. 104)

tectonic plate—a large block of lithosphere (p. 93)

testis—the male reproductive organ where sperm are produced (p. 40)

tissue—a groups of cells that work together for a specific job (p. 40)

transform boundary—the location where two tectonic plates slide past each other (p. 93)

transpiration—the loss of water from the leaves of plants (p. 72)

ureter—the tube that connects the kidney to the urinary bladder (p. 40)

urethra—the tube that leads from the urinary bladder to the outside of the body (p. 40)

uterus—the site where a fertilized egg develops into a fetus (p. 40)

velocity—the speed in a particular direction (p. 18)

volcano—an opening in Earth where magma is released (p. 93)

volume—the amount of space taken up, or occupied, by an object (p. 7)

Answer Key

Assessment, pp. 5-6

1. B	**2.** B	**3.** A	**4.** C
5. B	**6.** B	**7.** A	**8.** B
9. C	**10.** A	**11.** D	**12.** A
13. C	**14.** B	**15.** D	**16.** C

Unit 1, Lesson 1
Review, pp. 11–12

1. B	**2.** D	**3.** C	**4.** C
5. B	**6.** D	**7.** A	

8. Yes. For example, two different liquids may have the same boiling point. However, two different substances do not have all the same physical properties. The two liquids may have different densities.

9. An increase in temperature indicates either a physical or chemical change. For example, adding solid sodium metal to water is an exothermic chemical change. Dissolving solid sodium hydroxide in water is an exothermic physical change.

Solubility, p. 13

1. cerium sulfate
2. approximately 80 grams
3. 40 grams
4. 160 grams
5. approximately 180 grams
6. 60°C
7. Yes. Each solid shows a different solubility at various temperatures. This information can be used to identify the solid.

Density, p. 14

1. 7.14 g/cm³
2. zinc
3. 110 grams
4. 40 cm³
5. Yes. Each substance has a different density. The information can be used to identify the substance.

Chemical Reactions, p. 15

1. formula
2. created; destroyed
3. exothermic
4. product
5. equation
6. endothermic
7. reactivity
8. reactant
9. atoms
10. conservation

Experiment: Conservation of Mass, p. 17
Results and Analysis

1. Gas bubbles were produced.
2. Answers will vary.
3. Answer should be the same or very close to the value in question 2.

Conclusion

Mass is conserved during a chemical reaction.

Unit 1, Lesson 2
Review, p. 22

1. D	**2.** A	**3.** D	**4.** B	**5.** A	**6.** A

7. Upon impact, a person's body is still in motion. Without an airbag, a person's head will hit against the steering wheel.

8. Acceleration depends on mass. With a much smaller mass, a car accelerates with less force.

9. The table exerts an equal and opposite force against your hand.

Motion, p. 23

1. 4 m/10 s = 0.4 m/s
2. 2 m/5 s = 0.4 m/s
3. 2 m/2 s = 1 m/s
4. The squirrel did not move.
5. The line would slope downward.

A Roller-Coaster Ride, p. 24

1. B	**2.** C	**3.** A	**4.** D

A Newtonian Crossword Puzzle, p. 25
Across

5. acceleration
7. reaction
8. first
9. apple

10. gravity   **11.** third

13. second

Down

1. force   **2.** newton

3. inertia   **4.** increases

6. velocity   **8.** friction

12. push

Experiment: Acceleration Due to Gravity, pp. 27–28

Results and Analysis

1. Results will vary depending on the height of the drop point.

2. Results will vary but should be approximately 32 f/s² or 9.8 m/s².

Conclusions

1. All objects have the same acceleration due to gravity.

2. Results will vary but should be approximately 32 f/s² or 9.8 m/s².

3. The stopwatch may not have been started exactly when the ball was dropped or stopped when it landed. This would affect the time. Air resistance is also a factor.

Unit 1, Lesson 3

Review, pp. 33-34

1. B   **2.** C   **3.** D   **4.** A

5. C   **6.** B   **7.** C

8. Both convert a small amount of mass into an enormous amount of energy.

9. Both require activation energy to get started.

Chemical Reactions and Energy I, p. 35

1. exothermic reaction; the products have less energy than the reactants

2.
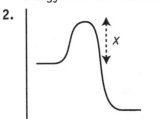

3.
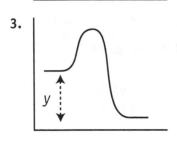

4.
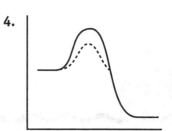

Chemical Reactions and Energy II, p. 36

1. endothermic; the product has more energy than the reactants

2. the reactants

3. the product

4.

A Long Voyage, p. 37

1. The plutonium cannot be used to make nuclear weapons.

2. If the space probe crashes, the plutonium will be released in chunks and not as a powder.

3. nuclear → heat → electricity

4. Both release radiation that can be stopped by a piece of paper.

Experiment: A Model of Nuclear Fission, p. 39

1. approximately half

2. 10 seconds

Conclusion

Pennies can be used to model how a radioactive substance decays based on its half-life.

Unit 2, Lesson 4

Review, pp. 44–45

1. B   **2.** D   **3.** C   **4.** C   **5.** A

6. Yes. The ovaries are an example. They function as part of both the reproductive and endocrine systems.

7. The cerebrum is most highly developed as it functions in thinking, reasoning, and memory.

8. Endocrine glands function by producing hormones that travel in the blood to their target organ, which can be located in another part of the body.

When the Kidneys Don't Work, p. 46

1. A dialysis machine filters wastes from the blood.
2. A kidney transplant is necessary when a person's kidneys have totally stopped functioning, and dialysis is not an option.
3. Yes. One kidney is adequate to filter the blood as Robert Herrick proved.

Hormones and Reproduction, p. 47

1. The testosterone level remains constant. The estrogen level fluctuates.
2. The estrogen is preparing the uterus should fertilization occur.
3. Usually only one egg is matured every 28 days. In contrast, sperm are continuously being produced and thus require a constant level of testosterone.
4. The estrogen levels would not change in the same way because the menstrual cycle ceases during pregnancy.

The Endocrine System, p. 48

1. Yes. The pineal gland regulates sleep patterns.
2. adrenal gland
3. pancreas and thyroid gland
4. Males have testes, while females have ovaries.
5. pancreas
6. thymus

Experiment: The Nervous System, p. 50

Results and Analysis

1. Answers will vary.
2. Answers will vary.
3. The hand should contain more sense receptors as it comes in contact with environmental stimuli much more frequently that the leg.

Conclusion

The hand contains numerous nerve cells that detect temperature and pressure

Unit 2, Lesson 5

Review, p. 55

1. A   2. D   3. C   4. B   5. C   6. A
7. Natural reproduction occurs without any human intervention or manipulation. In contrast, genetic engineering occurs only as the result of human manipulation.
8. about 70 million bases per chromosome

9. A mutation may occur in the DNA, but the DNA may not be making any RNA. Therefore, the effect will not be seen.

DNA Replication, p. 56

C-A-A-G-T-T-G-C-G-A-T-T-C-C-A-T-G-G

RNA Transcription, p. 57

C-A-A-G-U-U-G-C-G-A-U-U-C-C-A-U-G-G

Protein Synthesis, p. 58

glutamine—valine—alanine—isoleucine—proline—tryptophan

Mutations, p. 59

1. Answers will vary.
2. Answers will vary.
3. Answers will vary.
4. Answers will vary.
5. Most amino acids are coded for by two, three, and even four three-letter combinations. Therefore, changing one letter may not result in a different amino acid. For example, GCU, GCC, GCA, and GCG all specify the amino acid alanine. Therefore, changing the last base will not have any effect.

Experiment: Extracting DNA, p. 61

Results and Analysis

Long threads should collect on the skewer. These threads are DNA molecules.

Conclusion

The DNA can be extracted from the cells of an organism.

Unit 2, Lesson 6

Review, p. 66

1. B   2. D   3. A   4. B   5. D   6. C
7. In dim light, mainly the rods are stimulated. The cones must be stimulated to see colors.
8. The brain must receive information, or be given feedback, before it can direct the appropriate response.

Focusing the Light, p. 67

1. The eyeball of a nearsighted person is somewhat elongated, causing the light to focus on a point in front of the retina. Glasses must bend the light outward so that it focuses farther back on the retina.

2. The eyeball of a farsighted person is somewhat flattened, causing the light to focus on a point behind the retina. Glasses must bend the light inward so that it focuses more forward on the retina.

3. This is muscle tissue. These muscles change the shape of the lens in order to focus light onto the retina.

Mathematics and the Senses, p. 68

1. about 0.2 miles per second
2. 1000 signals
3. about 95 million miles away
4. 0.2 second
5. 90 pounds

It Doesn't Smell Anymore!, p. 69

1. A person may not smell a gas leak or smoke and recognize there is a fire.
2. nasal obstruction, breathing allergies, and nasal congestion
3. Repeated blows to the head destroyed olfactory cells.
4. As a person gets older, the ability to smell decreases.

Experiment: What Do You Taste?, p. 71

Results and Analysis
1. Answers will vary.   **2.** Answers will vary.
Conclusion
Color added to food may influence the taste a person detects.

Unit 2, Lesson 7

Review, p. 77
1. C   **2.** D   **3.** B   **4.** D
5. A   **6.** B   **7.** D
8. Limiting factors determine the maximum number of organisms that a population can contain.
9. Humans carry out respiration and combustion, which are two processes that add carbon dioxide to the atmosphere.

A Population and Ecosystem Crossword Puzzle, p. 78

Across
3. nitrogen   **5.** photosynthesis
11. carrying capacity   **12.** population
13. transpiration

Down
1. ecosystem   **2.** biotic factor
4. evaporation   **6.** respiration
7. soil   **8.** combustion
9. carbon   **10.** water cycle

Population Growth, p. 79

1. around day 5
2. about 65 paramecia/mL
3. space
4. The population will slowly start to decline in size as organisms die from lack of food.
5. The population will increase in size and reach a new carrying capacity.
6. The population will fluctuate close to its current carrying capacity.

The Carbon Cycle, p. 80

1. There has been a steady increase in the carbon dioxide concentration in the atmosphere.
2. With more plants in spring and summer, there is more photosynthetic activity. This increased activity uses more carbon dioxide.
3. With fewer plants in fall and winter, there is less photosynthetic activity. This decreased activity results in less carbon dioxide use.
4. The graph should show a steady increase in Earth's average temperature over time.

Experiment: Estimating the Size of a Population, p. 82

Analysis and Results
1. Answers will vary.
2. Possible answers include repeat the procedure and mark more beans to include in the population for recapture.
Conclusion
It's possible to use the mark-recapture method to estimate the size of a population.

Unit 2, Lesson 8

Review, p. 87
1. B   **2.** C   **3.** D   **4.** A   **5.** B   **6.** C
7. Those organisms with adaptations to the environment are more likely to survive and reproduce.
8. overproduction, variations, struggle to survive, successful reproduction

9. Darwin could not explain how traits were inherited and how variations arose among the members of a species.

The Galápagos Finches, p. 88

1. Beak size increased during dry years. One possible answer is that longer beaks were an adaptation needed to get insects that were deeper in twigs and rocks during the dry weather.
2. Beak size decreased during the wet year. One possible answer is that shorter, thicker beaks were an adaptation needed to break open seeds that were more plentiful during the wet year.
3. Because beak size did not change during 1981, a reasonable inference is that it was neither a dry nor wet year.

Weight as an Adaptation, p. 89

1. about 7 pounds
2. about 7 pounds
3. Babies with low birth weights may have body parts that are not functioning normally or may be more susceptible to diseases.
4. No. The graph shows that as infant weight increases above 7 pounds, the probability of death starts to increase.

Another Theory of Evolution, p. 90

1. Darwin stated that evolution was a slow or gradual process.
2. Punctuated equilibrium states that evolution has long periods where little or no changes occur interrupted by sudden and dramatic changes in a species.
3. Yes. Natural selection happens at times, while punctuated equilibrium occurs at other times. In addition, some species may be more likely to evolve through natural selection, while others evolve through punctuated equilibrium.

Experiment: Natural Selection, p. 92

Results and Analysis
Answers will vary.

Conclusion
Organisms that blend in with their environment have an adaptation. They are more likely to avoid being eaten by predators. As a result, they will survive and reproduce. Over time, their numbers will increase.

Unit 3, Lesson 9

Review, p. 97
1. D 2. A 3. C 4. B 5. D 6. C
7. The asthenosphere consists of molten rocks and is fluid. The lithosphere consists of solid rock and is divided into tectonic plates.
8. Oceanic crust is denser and thinner than continental crust.
9. Folded mountains form at convergent boundaries. Mid-ocean ridges form at divergent boundaries. Therefore, folded mountains do not form at mid-ocean ridges.

Tectonic Plates, p. 98

1. divergent boundary; mid-ocean ridges
2. The Andes Mountains are folded mountains formed at a convergent boundary between the Nazca plate and the South American plate.
3. The fastest-forming divergent boundary is found between the Pacific plate and the Nazca plate. The illustration shows that these two plates are moving 17.2 cm apart from one another each year.

Complete the Sentences, p. 99

1. volcano
2. mantle
3. convergent boundary
4. fault
5. transform boundary
6. lithosphere
7. tectonic plate
8. asthenosphere
9. divergent boundary
10. magma

Seismic Waves, p. 100

1. The lithosphere is the least dense because the wave speed is the slowest.
2. The mesosphere is the densest because the wave speed is the fastest.
3. The outer core is liquid because the wave speed is slower than through the inner core, which must be solid.
4. between 18.8 seconds and 21.4 seconds (150/8 and 150/7)

The Richter Scale, p. 101

1. 4.5
2. 10 mm
3. 90 mm (100 mm - 10 mm)

4. Each unit of magnitude represents a ten-fold increase in the maximum height of a wave on a seismogram. This can be seen most clearly at magnitude values between 3 and 5.

Experiment: Convection Currents, p. 103

Results and Analysis

Arrows should show two convection currents in the baking dish. There are two upward flows above the flame. Each upward flow then moves toward an end of the dish. Then there is a downward flow and a return horizontal flow toward the center. The cycle then continues.

Conclusion

Heating the oil decreases its density causing it to rise to the surface. At the surface, the oil cools as it flows to the ends of the dish. As it cools, it sinks and then flows to the center of the dish again to begin another cycle. Therefore, the oil and thyme represent a model of a convection current.

Unit 3, Lesson 10

Review, p. 108

1. B   2. C   3. D   4. A   5. D   6. C
7. No. For example, during a new moon, the half we do not see is in sunlight.
8. This planet is 5.74 times farther than Earth from the sun.

The Moon's Orbit, p. 109

1. B   2. A   3. D   4. A   5. C

Kepler's Laws, p. 110

1. Mars, because its orbit most closely resembles an ellipse.
2. Mars will be traveling the fastest between 2 and 4 because it is closest to the sun during this time.
3. Mercury has the shortest semimajor axis because it is closest to the sun.

Squeeze Gently, p. 111

1. C   2. B   3. D

The Sun, p. 112

1. The more mass a star has, the shorter its lifetime.
2. 5.4 billion years (10 billion − 4.6 billion)
3. 1650-1715 because there was no sunspot activity indicating the temperatures on Earth were cold
4. around 1950 because of the increased sunspot activity

Experiment: Calculating the Distance to the Sun, p. 114

Results and Analysis

1. Answers will vary.   2. Answers will vary.

Conclusion

A device to measure the distance between Earth and the sun can be constructed from ordinary materials.

Answer Key
Science 8, SV 9781419034367

4500783407-0607-2019

Printed in the U.S.A